Unfaithful

TRANSLATED BY

Translated By is a series dedicated to promoting translators' perspectives on their contributions to literary production, networks, and histories. It prioritizes writing by translators on translation, recognizing their creative and intellectual activity, and expands titles available in English about translation. The title of the series makes up for all the times the words "Translated by" were left off the cover of a book or excluded from literary history, and its incompleteness epitomizes the essential role of the translator in the making of literature. Overall, this series creates a space for translators to be recognized for the full range of their activity in literary networks.

SERIES EDITORS

Regina Galasso, University of Massachusetts Amherst, USA
Mario Pereira, University of Massachusetts Dartmouth, USA

ADVISORY BOARD

Aron Aji, University of Iowa, USA
Anna Elliott-Zielinska, Boston University, USA
Mara Faye Lethem, University of St Andrews, Spain
Adalberto Müller, Universidade Federal Fluminense, Brazil
Samantha Schnee, Words Without Borders, USA

VOLUMES IN THE SERIES
Unfaithful: A Translator's Memoir
Suzanne Jill Levine

Unfaithful

A Translator's Memoir

Suzanne Jill Levine

BLOOMSBURY ACADEMIC
NEW YORK • LONDON • OXFORD • NEW DELHI • SYDNEY

BLOOMSBURY ACADEMIC
Bloomsbury Publishing Inc
1385 Broadway, New York, NY 10018, USA
50 Bedford Square, London, WC1B 3DP, UK
29 Earlsfort Terrace, Dublin 2, Ireland

BLOOMSBURY, BLOOMSBURY ACADEMIC and the Diana logo are trademarks of
Bloomsbury Publishing Plc

First published in the United States of America 2025

Cover design: Eleanor Rose
Cover photo provided by the author

Bloomsbury Publishing Inc does not have any control over, or responsibility for,
any third-party websites referred to or in this book. All internet addresses given in
this book were correct at the time of going to press. The author and publisher regret
any inconvenience caused if addresses have changed or sites have ceased to exist,
but can accept no responsibility for any such changes.

A catalog record for this book is available from the Library of Congress.

ISBN: HB: 979-8-7651-3372-9
         PB: 979-8-7651-3373-6
         ePDF: 979-8-7651-3375-0
         eBook: 979-8-7651-3374-3

Series: Translated By

Typeset by RefineCatch Limited, Bungay, Suffolk
Printed and bound in the United States of America

To find out more about our authors and books visit www.bloomsbury.com
and sign up for our newsletters.

Contents

Figures

Foreword

Visiting the past is a chance to enlighten and perhaps lighten the present. History and my story cross paths beginning in the era of the Cuban revolution and unfolding in New York City in the turbulent 1960s and 1970s and beyond. The political turmoil around the revolution, a mere ninety miles south of Key West, fomented worldwide interest not only in Cuba but in all of Latin America—and, on the literary front, prestigious presses in Paris and in New York were suddenly eager to discover and to publish the great poets and masters of fiction, among them Jorge Luis Borges, Julio Cortázar and Pablo Neruda, as well as Gabriel García Márquez and a cast of new writers like Manuel Puig and Guillermo Cabrera Infante, from Cuba and Mexico to Brazil and Argentina. This literary goldmine was popularly called "the Boom." As a young translator I had the good fortune of "being there."

Suzanne Jill Levine
Santa Barbara, 2024

Part One

Close Encounters

Prologue: The Latin American Boom

In 1967 I was a graduate student at age twenty at Columbia University, where I initially intended to major in International Studies with a specialization in Latin American Studies. In the early 1960s President Kennedy, with progressive initiatives such as the Peace Corps, was urging young people to go out into the developing countries of the world as missionaries of peace or emissaries of democracy, naïve as all that seems now. South America was a key continent for students of Spanish to carry "the torch" of progress. With the Cuban Revolution and Castro's trumpeted literacy campaign began an era in which the southern hemisphere was a strategic region in the Cold War—with Soviet war machines installed only ninety miles away on the island of Cuba.

As part of my graduate studies, I traveled to Colombia in the summer of 1968 where I discovered a newly published book, *Cien años de soledad*. This was the now legendary and hyperbolic saga *One Hundred Years of Solitude*, an exciting epic satire (I couldn't put the book down until I reached the last page) which helped convince me to stay on a literary path. My timing corresponded to the rise of what literary critic Luis Harss baptized as the "Boom," referring to a new post-World War Two generation of extraordinary writers from all over Latin America who were emerging, many of whom wrote their most influential novels from exile, like Argentine Julio Cortázar's *Hopscotch* and Peruvian Mario Vargas Llosa's *The Green House*. Gabriel García Márquez, the Cuban Guillermo Cabrera Infante, the Argentine Manuel Puig were among many other writers from diverse South American countries, from the Caribbean to the Southern Cone, in most cases fleeing persecution or political tyranny.

Twentieth-century avant-garde literature and arts had found new life not only south of the border but in exile. Paris became Cortázar's refuge in exile, as Barcelona became the same for Colombian García Márquez and Peruvian Vargas Llosa. Europe and North America re-discovered the Caribbean and Central and South America, and Jorge Luis Borges, Carlos Fuentes, Gabriel García Márquez, Julio Cortázar and Mario Vargas Llosa were the first Latin Americans to become literary figures on a new world stage. Facing in the 1970s right-wing dictators and the infamous "dirty wars" in Argentina, Uruguay and Chile, these writers transcended regionalism, reinventing their literature out of their non-Western as well as Spanish and European heritage and the impact of North America, as thirsty readers of John Dos Passos, Camus, Sartre, James Joyce, Kafka, Virginia Woolf, Hemingway and Faulkner, Flaubert, and Henry James.

Politics and art went hand in hand, as in the inventions of magical realism, which cast both a cosmic and a satirical lens on the catastrophic consequences of colonialism and political corruption. Indigenous beliefs and transplanted African cultures, European Surrealism and modernism were watershed influences subtly and not so subtly woven into the groundbreaking *One Hundred Years of Solitude*, the book I would decide to tackle for my M.A. thesis. But the narrative revolution was preceded by early twentieth-century poetic movements like Borges's "Ultraism" and Vicente Huidobro's "Creationism," poetry that revolutionized the Spanish language. By the 1960s two Latin Americans had harvested Nobel prizes, the first going to Chilean woman poet Gabriela Mistral and a few years later, to a magical realist novelist from Guatemala, Miguel Angel Asturias. Others would follow: Pablo Neruda (Chile, 1972), García Márquez (Colombia, 1984), Octavio Paz (Mexico, 1990), and Vargas Llosa (Peru, 2017). Latin American literature had finally stepped up to center stage.

According to the iconic Julio Cortázar, el Boom ended in the mid-1970s with the dirty wars and brutal dictatorships, and in many ways he was right. In the 1960s and 1970s in Europe and the Americas, along with the Beatles, radical politics and pop art, writing was bursting with philosophical, experimental and artistic new twists. South American novelists and poets were the next wave, a new avant-garde, reinterpreting mythologies, penetrating complex social realities, and inventing an authentically Latin American literary language that moved beyond the earlier trend of regionalist literature which still reinforced the florid style of traditional Spanish rhetoric from centuries past. The rich variations of speech and language in the different regions of South America and Spain were essential to what made the new Latin American writing original. Translating creatively subversive Cabrera Infante and Manuel Puig, taking on the task of making spoken Cuban and Argentine into a new literary language in translation, was my true entry into the world of writing. Before working with them, everything had been a rehearsal.

1

Beginnings

If my parents hadn't died when they did, I doubt that I would have ever left the city to go away to college. I grew up in the 1950s in a New York Jewish American family of limited means. I was the youngest of four, almost a generation younger than my siblings, and we lived in the close quarters of a two-bedroom apartment, between Washington Heights and Inwood, thirty blocks south of the northern tip of Manhattan. My family lived in the Heights from my birth to 1963, when it was mainly a neighborhood of Jews, Irish, Italians, Greeks and recent European refugees from the Second World War (one of the most famous or infamous being Henry Kissinger). The world-class dancer Jacques D'Amboise also came from the 'hood, and later it became the Dominican territory of Lin-Manuel Miranda's hit musical "In the Heights." These days, of course, Washington Heights is gentrified, and those big apartments with their high ceilings are in high demand.

Like many "native" New Yorkers, in my twenties I never considered living anywhere else except of course cosmopolitan meccas like Paris or London. My inner map of the United States sort of resembled Saul Steinberg's famous New Yorker cartoon where he depicts New York as separated from the rest of the country sketched out as an undefined expanse located west of the Hudson River. While I am no Freud, I suspect that living as a small child in an apartment in close quarters with my brother and sisters, very attractive young adults who were somewhere between siblings and parental figures to me, might have nurtured my bisexual leanings. As the queer revolution had not yet happened, "bisexual" was the definition that seemed to fit me though I wouldn't recognize this reality until my early thirties.

The one advantage as the youngest of my family was that I belonged to the Sixties, a more progressive era, when girls were supposed to be as well educated as boys to have more fulfilling lives and to make the world better. It was no longer acceptable not to educate girls, and unlike my sisters, I was expected, like my peers, to seek a college education.

When I had started French at twelve in Junior High P.S. 52 back in the late 1950s, I took to language class like a duck to *sauce à l'orange*. We had a perversely witty male teacher with a British accent who reminded me of the actor Alastair Sims, the one who played with intelligent irony a comically neurotic Scrooge in the 1950s film version of *A Christmas Carol*. I was captivated by how speaking another language allowed me to be someone else, to bring forth a part of myself that seemed to express itself more fully in the other language.

Early dreams of escaping to the exotic splendors of Europe, preferably Rome or Paris or somewhere in the Mediterranean, were kindled not only by the riches of History, but also by the glamourous images devoured at the Hollywood movies I went to every Saturday night as a kid accompanying my parents. They took me because they couldn't afford a babysitter, and they didn't seem to notice that some of the films were only for a mature audience. Saturday excursions to the RKO theater palace on 181st or to the Dyckman Street movie house, or simply nights in front of the TV provided mesmerizing entertainment. *Million Dollar Movie* (on Channel 9, I think) was the first movie channel, with its romantic musical theme from *Gone with the Wind*. On this channel I first became acquainted with those Hollywood films that were or were about to become "classics."

No less enjoyable were the times after supper when we gathered around the Zenith television—not aware of how primitive and small the screen was—to laugh with Sid Caesar on his *Show of Shows* or the zany Groucho Marx and his duck announcing the secret word in *You Bet Your Life*, Desi and dizzy Lucy in *I Love Lucy*, George Burns and his infallible GracieAllen, and the perfectly poker-faced Jack Benny. Just to see Benny's speechless slightly fey and deadpan response, or to watch Groucho, cigar in mouth, eyeing the public while uttering a quip, was enough to bring out the giggles and guffaws.

It's not hard to understand movie mania in my family. Movies were, from the early days, an escape for everyone everywhere, poor or rich, from the tedium or worries of real life. Also, the entertainment business, especially before the Second World War, was one of the few careers open to Jews. Speaking of difficult times of my family back in the 1920s, my mother Lena, along with her brothers and sisters and her parents, moved from a boarding house in Philadelphia to 122nd Street and Park Avenue in New York, where her youngest sister, my aunt Gertie, was born. In Manhattan, or more specifically in Harlem, the family of nine lived in what was called a railroad apartment. New York has always been a city of constant changes; Harlem was a Jewish ghetto before it became predominantly an African American 'hood and Puerto Rican barrio.

Names were Americanized, that is, translated. When she was only forty-eight, my grandmother named Elke, from Frankfurt they said, became Ida in New York, and sadly died of a stroke or high blood pressure, not sure which. (From a family that retained few remnants of its now remote origins, I came from a translated world as, in a way, do all exiles or immigrants.) My elders had transmigrated themselves into New Yorkers, grateful to America for saving them from persecution and worse in Europe. For them this seemed a good thing, the only way to survive. They had neither time nor inclination to examine how exile produces alienation, or mental roadblocks that compensate for some loss. They barely even bothered to rescue any memories of their lost origins. My father Meyer was called Mike, and my mom's name Lena changed to Elaine probably when she started working, or when she lost her mother Ida, the person she loved and needed most. Despite having older brothers and a mysterious older sister, she had to take over, take care of the younger ones in her family because her father was a philanderer who didn't provide for his family and was almost never home leaving my mother at age seventeen to take care of her siblings.

Mom and her siblings were still crowded together in that apartment overlooking the elevated subway tracks on 122nd Street near Park Avenue when, in the 1920s, she met my father. At the time he was working for my paternal grandfather Sam, who, I am guessing, was a slum landlord. As no one is left to tell me, guessing—or "interpreting"—is the best I can do. And so, doing his father's bidding, my dad had come knocking on doors to receive the month's rent. He was twenty-eight years old and fell head over heels in love with the nineteen-year-old raven-haired beauty who opened the door, the girl who would be my mother.

*

When I was eight or nine, I had started piano lessons with a German refugee who lived near us. From the start I had potential, it seemed, or as an old Frenchman exclaimed many years later, I had "le feu sacré." After a couple of years, my first piano teacher was the one who recommended that my parents take me to Julliard. When the time came for the audition, my father dutifully took me downtown to the famous music school. Armed with my sacred fire, I passed the scholarship audition at Juilliard's Prep Division and one year later another audition to attend the High School of Music & Art, in 1960. Both these fine schools had high standards. Music & Art produced an extraordinary list of musicians, artists, composers, actors and intellectuals like my fellow 1963 graduate Leon Botstein, the distinguished president of Bard College; and Juilliard needs no introduction.

I didn't have what it takes, however, to practice ten hours a day and face huge audiences, so my future wasn't the concert hall. Still, my Baldwin console piano has always moved with me, scratched up as it is by so many displacements, and from time to time it is still a pleasure to be able to play favorite pieces I learned so long ago.

*

It was before my sixteenth birthday, during senior year at Music & Art, when my mother suddenly had convulsions. Ten weeks later, on New Year's Day, she died of a malignant brain tumor, one month shy of her fifty-seventh birthday. This sad catastrophe was like a rug that had been pulled from under me. That New Year's Day of 1963, I was supposed to go to a movie with a boy I knew from summers with my sister at the beach, Neil Baldwin. I called him that morning to postpone our chaste date, but it seemed unspeakable, so final to say the words "my mother died." Because I knew Neil studied French as I did, I repeated the first words "Aujourd'hui, maman est morte" from Albert Camus's *The Stranger*. I wouldn't learn until years later the name of the cancer that killed her, glioblastoma, which is still incurable, though more treatable than it was in 1963.

My mother would always be a bit enigmatic to me; I was just beginning to know her when she passed. I loved her, her warm presence, her lively sense of humor, her being there, but didn't get a chance to really know her, that is, from an adult perspective. The trauma that had happened to my mother when she lost her mother at seventeen, had now happened to me at sixteen. As if destined to repeat her fate as a quasi-orphan, I felt stranded just as my mom must have felt at the same age. There were school events where every girl had her mother with her except for me. But I had the good fortune to have my kind and beautiful eldest sister Alice, who, with four kids of her own, would be like a mother to me. Less than two years later in September 1964 when I was beginning sophomore year of college, before my eighteenth birthday, my father died even more abruptly, from a heart attack, a broken heart really.

*

I was not your typical Vassar girl, certainly not a debutante. When it came time to choose a college, my brother-in-law and my father were very concerned that I get the best education. Aside from its prestige as one of the "seven sisters,"

Barnard would cost less since I could live at home. On Saturdays, I'd take the subway from home to 116th Street and Broadway to go to my piano lesson and theory class at Juilliard, located a few blocks away; I loved to take the shortcut through the Barnard campus with its old ivy-covered stone walls. For me at that time Barnard's yard was like an enchanted garden.

My brother-in-law Ben urged me to apply to Vassar College, as it was very competitive for native New Yorkers to get into Barnard. Vassar seemed out of range for Jewish kids, especially lower-middle-class Jews, so I was reluctant to apply. At the High School of Music & Art, my grades in French, English and music were fine with an average around 90, but I wasn't an all-around star student. As it turned out, Vassar was a better choice, because with Mom gone, home was no longer home, like that song that says a house is not a home. Our modest rental apartment was a secure haven when my mother lived, but without her warm vibrant presence, that apartment was an empty shell. We all seemed to agree that the best thing for me was to go away to college, away from the city.

I believe Vassar accepted me as what today would be called a "diverse" candidate because of my musical background, and, curiously, my modest model career. Ironically my mother's rather naïve American belief in show biz as a road to success seemed to have enhanced my profile as a bright young student with good grades. My mother—always the down-to-earth pragmatist, who once exclaimed that someone was a "fool with a Ph.D."—never appeared to have qualms about taking me out of school to model, and as it turns out, the admissions interviewer at Vassar was impressed that I had modeled for *American Girl*, the official Girl Scout magazine. The admissions process to high-ranking colleges was sensitive to candidates who, aside from high grades, had special talents, interests, backgrounds like, for example, knowing how to play a musical instrument.

Girls and even boys normally were accompanied by parents on their college visit for the admissions interview. Dad had to work and was a sad shadow of his former self, after Mom died. The logical companion would have been Alice the eldest, but she had her hands full as the mother of four kids. Thus, only two months after Mom died, in early March 1963, I took the commuter train with the Hudson River as my sole companion, all the way up to the depressing looking city of Poughkeepsie; this was the furthest I had ever traveled alone, and now I was about to enter college at age sixteen.

When the businesslike middle-aged interviewer greeted me with a friendly, "Hello, are you Suzanne?" I replied, "I am, though people call me Jill as my family always called me by my middle name." She accepted that information with good humor and invited me to sit facing her in comfortable armchairs in a far corner of the grand salon. This straightlaced environment, far from gritty New York and the warm lively world of my family, felt alien, but the interviewer seemed, to my relief, to be encouraging. "So, I see you have an impressive background in music. Do you plan to continue studying piano here at Vassar?" "After my mother died," I said, "I had to quit Juilliard, so I am really glad to have the chance here at Vassar to return to the piano and study music." I somehow mustered up the confidence or must have given off a confident air: the surprising acceptance letter came a month or two later.

*

College in the 1960s, compared to these days, had more rigorous requirements in the liberal arts, and we were required to know not only one but a second and sometimes even a third foreign language. French gave me a head start to acquire other Romance languages with greater ease, and because of my head start with French, in high school I was thinking of a career at the United Nations as an interpreter. The UN had a lot of prestige, and there was the glamorous Audrey Hepburn as an interpreter in *Charade* or the striking Hitchcockian images of the UN in *North by Northwest*.[1] My UN fantasy quickly faded upon learning more about the polyglot requirements and the rigorous tedium of this highly technical skill.

I chose Spanish, or perhaps Spanish chose me, a pragmatic path of least resistance as it was considered a relatively easy language to learn—and as I was in the infirmary with mononucleosis, "the kissing disease," for the first two weeks of classes, this seemed a good choice. My first Spanish professor, the affable Sr. Del Rio, dapper, gray-haired, meticulous, a no-nonsense Vassar teacher with a clear Castilian accent, was far more welcoming than the tense young French instructor teaching my freshman French class. She seemed aloof and cold. Now, having been a teacher for many years, I realize that as a newcomer she must have been nervous, and I almost feel a retrospective sympathy. In any case the Spanish teachers seemed livelier, and while rigorous, less judgmental, with more *joie de vivre*, ironically, than the French.

I chose Spanish as my major by a process of elimination, a doubtlessly common method among students. Our class advisor, the decadent-looking Italian teacher Mr. Domandi with his pock-marked face, whose name sounded in Italian like a cross between "tomorrow" and "Sunday," tilted the scale with one compelling reason. Known to be flirtatious, Mr. Domandi confirmed my impression that Spanish was more "practical" in today's world. I sensed, of course, that the Italian professor considered French and Italian culture superior to Spanish, and I had the same unspoken prejudice. My earlier awareness of Hispanic culture had been limited to few comic moments on TV shows, like Ricky Ricardo on *I Love Lucy*. This bird's eye view of Hispanic culture would grow into admiration at college where I would read great literary works. Another plus of majoring in a Romance language—maybe the most compelling reason for a student with modest means—was the opportunity to spend junior year in a foreign country.

As I already knew French, Spanish grammar was relatively easy to grasp, and Spanish pronunciation, relative to French, was user friendly, with its straightforward vocalization of the five vowels. Spanish is a phonetic language, accessible in that it sounds just as it is spelled. Which often is not the case with English as well as French, about which Argentine writer Borges—obliged to learn French as a teenager because he and his family were stuck in Geneva, Switzerland during "the Great War," World War One—quipped with his mischievous irony: "The French, les pauvres, all they have is the 'u.'"

Aside from the rich diversity of spoken Spanish, especially in the regions of South America, there were of course a few formidable challenges in Spanish, like learning to roll one's double r's as in "ferrocarril," the word for railroad—the trick was to bend your head down, loosen your tongue and press it against the roof of your mouth. What is certain is that I learned more Spanish in freshman year at Vassar College than I had French during four years at junior high and high school. The extra hour per week in college at the language laboratory, an intense practice of listening and repeating, conquering the challenges of pronunciation, had a lot to do with this rapid acquisition.

*

My senior year at Vassar College in 1966–67 included a whole semester devoted meticulously to *Don Quixote*, masterpiece of the Spanish Golden Age and of world literature, generally considered the first modern novel. At the same time, I was studying contemporary Latin American literature, taught by Raúl Silva Cáceres, a young Chilean professor. And was already realizing that Latin America was probably more relevant than Spain, to my life as an American. I even thought that, by becoming a translator I would be among those international workers trying to create more positive relationship between the two hemispheres. The United States, we all know, exploited Latin America but especially Central

America and Cuba in fundamental ways that undermined the relationship between North and South.

Reading the Quixote, I would realize later, taught us how to read contemporary Latin American writers and vice versa. Again, it was Borges who would bring this rich dialogue into greater focus. Professor Cáceres gave off the air of a serious scholar, or at least a remote demeanor behind his glasses, unlike flirtatious Alfredo Matilla, who was popular with the girls mainly because he drove a green Morgan convertible sports car. The Chilean, on the other hand, seemed both professional and jittery—and indifferent to the girls—and we, insensitive as the young can be, made fun of his nervous tics. Cáceres compulsively would adjust his already tidy cufflinks before he began his lecture. Along with his Chilean hiss this jittery tic made some girls think he was gay, or, simply, that he drank lots of coffee. Susan Kingston, a very tall and droll classmate with a sharp sense of humor, who always referred to Paris as the "City of Lights," imitated Raúl's lisp and cufflink adjustments to perfection.

It was in his class that I probably first heard of "la literatura fantástica" and magical realism, and it was certainly the first time I remember hearing about Borges, mentioned along with an important critic in Paris named Emir Rodríguez Monegal. Like most notes one takes in college, Cáceres's passing reference to "Monegal" (of Catalan origins and not a usual surname in Spanish) during that class in my senior year went in one ear and quickly out the other. But, after Emir entered my life a couple of years later, I looked back at my college scribbles and realized I had first heard his name in Cáceres's class. Like one of those coincidences that life affords us, Emir was already a presence though I didn't know it at the time. Another synchronicity was that my teacher Dr. Cáceres and I would soon be fellow contributors to a scholarly volume published in 1977 on García Márquez's *One Hundred Years of Solitude*, in which I explored how *Pedro Páramo* by Mexican Juan Rulfo was an inspiring precedent for García Márquez's famous novel.

2

Living in Spanish

One often amusing pitfall during my first months in Spain was the embarrassment of uttering (unintentionally) something absurd or obscene in Spanish. "Pico" the word for "mountain" in Chile, for example, means "prick"; "concha" meaning seashell is slang in Argentina and Uruguay for the vagina; the Chilean word "guagua" means infant while in Cuba it means "bus" (derived from the English "wagon") so that if in a Chilean story a woman lifts up a baby, the same phrase read by a Cuban would mean that the woman was performing a herculean feat.

In late August 1965 I boarded my very first flight at Idlewild Airport—before the terminal became John F. Kennedy International Airport. My sister Alice and my brother Donny drove me to the airport and took me as far as the TWA gate, which you could do in those days before globe-trotting terrorism and, more recently, the pandemic. I had been anxious all summer about going up in an airplane, about my imminent departure faraway from family to the other side of the world for a whole year. When I stood hesitantly at the gate, my brother patted me on the shoulder to give me a gentle push, and, not looking back, I walked up the red carpeted ramp of the futuristic TWA tunnel to the plane. After I took my window seat and the plane moved onto the runway, my anxiety soon turned to amazement. I was thrilled by the speed, by the powerful jets that in minutes thrust us up into the sky, and by how, incredibly, in so few hours after nightfall, crossing the vast Atlantic for the first time, one could see out the tiny window a bright golden dawn break over cottony clouds, and then after crossing the ocean, the miracle of land below!

We landed in the early morning on the high plateau of Madrid, a city I knew only from a Spanish Civil War documentary, *To Die in Madrid*, and a 1950s star-studded Hollywood movie starring Tyrone Power and Ava Gardner, both gorgeous. The film was loosely based on Hemingway's post-war novella *The Sun Also Rises*. "The Sun Only Rises" would be the Cuban Cabrera Infante's pun or parody of the great Hemingway, alluding of course to the novella's plot, that is, the former soldier Jake's castration or impotence from a bullet wound.

I managed to articulate the address where I was going to the impressed taxi driver. Between the jetlag and the excitement of being in Spain, I also managed to engage in conversation and even to understand his fast chatter in his marvelously emphatic accent. As he dropped me and my suitcase on a wide sidewalk in front of the wrought iron entrance to an old apartment building on Ronda de Segovia, he said to me "soy tu primer novio en España!" announcing he was my very first boyfriend in Spain. His friendly openness reassured me as a young first-time traveler to a strange and wondrous land.

Those first days were so overwhelmingly foreign, utter otherness, almost like a dream, partly because of Madrid's altitude which made me sleepy by the afternoon, but also because I had traveled not only in space but back in time. Compared to New York, Madrid was a city from the Middle Ages, so different and distant, its people and their ways of being, the shops, the smells, the bars and cafés, the marvelously ornate buildings. In retrospect, elegant yet earthy Madrid was a perfect introduction to Europe.

I was eighteen going on nineteen, and like many students abroad I lived with a local family, supposedly for immersion in the language and culture, though foreign students were also a source of income. My home on Ronda de Segovia that academic year was the apartment of Valencian widow Joséfina Lopez García—most of the hosts or rather hostesses to my fellow students were widowed, it seemed, most of them by the infamous Civil War. The first day I arrived, or maybe the second, "Señora" Lopez García, also called "Doña" out of respect for her as a widow, took me shopping to a vast and noisy covered open-air market, and invited me to the white almond drink known as horchata. So common nowadays in taco stands, horchata was an exotic drink I had never encountered before, almost like a milkshake but with a refreshing taste of almond and cinnamon.

Like many New Yorkers I was provincial in that New York was the only place to live, but I was also a worldly young city dweller. I adapted to Madrid life, melting into the streets of the *madrileños*. My camouflage was not perfect, and not only because occasionally I wore slacks or jeans—Spanish women did not wear pants then—but also because people noticed when I wrote in my notebook while sitting on the bus. This was because I am left-handed or *zurda*. Being left-handed, especially in a Catholic country, was *siniestra*, sinister like Satan. In many countries, left-handed children often were retrained to write with their right hand, as had happened to my father in the Bronx where he grew up in the early 1900s. Maybe a partial explanation for his insecurity, I thought years later, after learning that forcing kids to change their dominant hand could cause them to stutter.

On weekday mornings, I would hop on a bus at the Puerta de Toledo stop, to go to the university in a more elegant part of town, unlike the working-class neighborhood of Ronda de Segovia where I lived, a hilly section beneath a great cathedral and not far from the river. Often the same mustachioed blue-eyed ticket seller was on the 33 bus that began its route at the Puerta de Toledo where I got on. I had an almost childish crush on him and appreciated how easily he smiled or mumbled some pleasant comment as I jumped on board. Friendly, spontaneous experiences like this were exhilarating and made me feel "native."

The bus would rumble from the busy, colorful and central Puerta del Sol to the more refined neighborhood of the Universidad Complutense, passing the palatial home of the famous Duchess of Alba who had modeled for Goya's *Naked Maja*. The double-decker buses, which apparently were imported from England, were fun to catch, and I would scramble up the steep narrow stairs to the top deck to grab a seat on the edge and watch from above the bustling city, people going to work in the mornings, food shops with huge hunks of pink ham and other stranger looking, darker meats on display, town criers selling lottery tickets "PARA HOY!" Women strolled typically locked arm in arm along the narrow sidewalks, and to get past them, you had to step into the street, careful to avoid rushing cars or looming buses.

At the university in Spain's capital my classes were of course in Spanish, or *castellano* as properly called, taught by local professors, some quite distinguished in their fields as historians or literary scholars. An outstanding course in art history, with a buoyant professor named Misol with lively eyes behind thick glasses, actually took place right in the Prado Museum, where, in front of the paintings themselves, Professor Misol hopped about, pointing and teaching us, stressing all that we could digest, about the Dutch and Flemish masters, the Italian Renaissance, the Spanish Baroque, and especially Velazquez and Goya—who I especially loved—and Caravaggio's chiaroscuro and Leonardo da Vinci, Durer and the mysterious Hieronymus Bosch. Bosch's monstrous *Garden of Earthly Delights* was a revelation like so much that we experienced, immersed in that precious and generous collection of pictorial treasures.

During the first semester I shared a room with a cheerful tall girl from Illinois named Judy, where we slept side by side in twin Murphy beds—which, each morning, were made and returned to their vertical wooden closet. The other two bedrooms belonged to the widow and her "spinster" daughter Alicia. I had the sense that Alicia, quiet, a student of medicine, looked upon us with mild disapproval, and, unlike her mother, didn't have a forced smile on her face. It even crossed my mind that Alicia might like women rather than men, but I never voiced this. She and her mother, a talkative, stocky, middle-aged lady whose Spanish was loud and clear, were polite enough and even included us in the midday Sunday *almuerzo* (the main meal of the day, much heavier than lunch back home) in which we were treated to an authentic Valencian paella.

Despite the evident hospitality, Judy and I felt that this was, logically, an economic arrangement for them, and that perhaps a certain falsity hovered over the "immersion" experience with families. Most nights their maid Agustina, a slight and very pale girl who seemed our age or maybe even younger, slept on a foldaway cot in the kitchen. Judy and I felt uncomfortable about this, but Agustina seemed to consider it normal. Unlike her boss she was warm and natural, serving us *café con leche* and *tostadas* (the typical Spanish breakfast), and we befriended Agustina with affection and good cheer, almost like sisters, under the sovereignty of Señora Doña Lopez García.

It was the fall of 1965, a time when Spain, so Catholic, still belonged to an almost medieval era, and still was a police state under Franco. Aside from the strong presence everywhere of poker-faced policemen, or the *guardia civil* in their three-cornered hats, there were severe regulations. I had an embarrassing encounter with Customs when a supply of birth control pills from a boyfriend in New York was mailed to me. I was called down to the Customs office. "Señorita, these are against the law in Spain!" I vowed innocence as the arrival of this "gift" from a strange friend was a surprise to me as well, and the infamous pills were sent back to my strange good Samaritan boyfriend—who had only been trying to facilitate what he had experienced as my hesitant sexual activity. Like many girls I was afraid of getting pregnant.

A bright side of Spain then was that global tourism had not yet trampled all over the country's major cities, although its Mediterranean shores were already overrun with Northern Europeans. Indeed, the term "global" was not used in those days. In a Catholic country where sex was forbidden until girls married, American and other foreign girls and women were very popular with the male population. The boys were aggressively on the prowl, which could often be unpleasant but, after Vassar, it was a big change, and I and the other girls literally could have dated a different boy almost every day of the week. In my case the boys didn't get too much past first base, mainly because of the threat of pregnancy which I greatly feared, but still, decent middle-class Spanish girls wouldn't even leave the dugout, so, as I said, we were popular.

This was the Madrid whose romantic version, as I mentioned, I had seen in the film Guillermo Cabrera Infante called *The Sun Only Rises* based on Hemingway's "lost generation" novella. A stunning diva of the 1940s and 1950s, Ava Gardner, so sexy with her curvaceous figure and cleft chin, in a hotel in Madrid, abandons or is abandoned by a young bullfighter lover, played by an inept but good-looking B actor named Robert Evans, who became a major producer in Hollywood (notably of *Chinatown* and of *The Godfather*). The romantic film ends unhappily, because the man she really loves, played by the handsome Tyrone Power (who really would die of a heart attack in his early forties after the film came out in 1952) can never be her lover. This movie of course had little to do with the reality of being in Madrid as a college student in 1966; nonetheless, the sexual dilemma and amorous obstacle found in me a sympathetic spectator.

"From Madrid to Heaven" or "De Madrid al Cielo" was a folksy refrain in praise of this capital city on a high plateau. Madrid was the traditional center of the Spanish-speaking world then, and my first foreign city. Many funny awkward moments occurred at the beginning, in a country so infused with a long complex history which, with only two years of college Spanish, I still barely knew. One funny anecdote from that first month concerns my brother Donny's visit to Madrid, on his way to Barcelona where he would spend his eye surgeon residency at the world-famous Barraquer clinic. He arrived in Madrid two weeks after I landed and, as he would continue almost immediately on to Barcelona, we decided to see all we could, the one full day he was with me in Madrid.

Both of us newcomers especially wanted to see a flamenco show, and so we got into a cab, I asked the driver to take us to flamenco, and he dropped us off at a place that had a huge restaurant and bar as well as a stage for the flamenco. The maître d' or whatever he was at the door looked at us with curiosity and I assumed it was because of our informal typical American clothes: I was wearing sandals and what was casually fashionable then, a madras wrap-around skirt; my brother didn't wear a jacket or tie. The maître d' seemed, for some strange reason, to take us under his wing and led us to the other end of the restaurant so that we could have a front seat, our table right against the railing overlooking the stage below.

As we had entered, we both noticed only single women at every table, very dressy and wearing lots of make-up. I asked Donny, "Why are all those women sitting alone?" to which he answered, "It must be between shows, and they are waiting for their husbands who went to the men's room." Was he pulling my leg or was he as naïve as myself? We were served the delicious traditional sangria and encouraged by the waiter to watch the show that was just beginning. The dancers' agility and strutting, the music's intensity, the colors of the costumes, the novelty of flamenco even in this commercial venue was thrilling, but when it was intermission, Donny said, suddenly in a rush, "We should leave now." Finally, it had dawned on him—a little slow on the uptake maybe from the jetlag? After we were in a taxi, he explained to me that this was a pick-up dive, and the women were call girls. We both felt embarrassed as we exited, "How could we be so dumb?" It was clear that the driver obviously took us there because he had an agreement with the brothel/bar-restaurant and assumed that we were naïve Americans.

The Spanish way of life had a different pace, followed a philosophy of *ocio*—which fascinated me as one of those words that couldn't be really translated. "Leisure" and "idleness" would be the closest, but *ocio* was both more carefree and more attentive to everyday life, almost an existential way of being that deliberately ignored time. Some of my fellow students from the U.S. started to complain, like me, about how slow or incredibly inefficient everything was in Spain. This was a foolish complaint on our part, our American naivete, or a simple lack of understanding of the foreign culture. Not only was there a major economic gap between the two countries which impacted everyday life, but we came from a country where time was money.

My new and handsome friend, blond, blue-eyed Curt Glick, was in tune with *ocio* but I wasn't, at least not enough. I was determined to immerse myself totally to learn, which meant, after a while, not spending too much time with my American classmates despite my attachment to this boy I met the first day of class. We were attracted to each other and soon began dating. Curt already spoke excellent Mexican Spanish from previous travels in Mexico, and I was happy to go places with him. But his Cary Grant wisecracks put me off even though I liked witty boys, and, typical of me, I didn't let my heart take over, something I would later regret. Curt hailed from the South, Jacksonville, Florida, hence seemed more suited or comfortable with *ocio*, and I was impressed by his experiences as a seasoned backpack traveler who had been in Mexico as well. It was foolish to make life a competition with men and their privilege, but I envied male freedom and longed for the excitement to venture forth on my own little adventures. Maybe that was the spunky New Yorker in me who dared to confront insecurity or innocence or, simply, the lack of experience.

In any case, that fall of 1965, Curt and I took day trips, the first one to hot dusty dreamy Aranjuez where I first encountered an encampment of Roma people (called gypsies then) and then, on another Sunday to the majestic El Escorial, and even week-long trips to romantic beach places like the island of Ibiza, where we bicycled to the tip of the island and my transistor radio captured music I had never heard before, the sounds of Northern Africa. Ibiza via Barcelona was our first long trip together in September and later in the winter we hitchhiked along the southern coast from Malaga to Algeciras where we caught a boat (called, apropos, *The Virgin of Africa*) to Tangiers. Our one night in Tangiers in a rundown hotel on a bed that sank in the middle was, alas, the only time I managed to set foot on Africa, and while Tangiers had a Kasbah and one ate delicious couscous, it was more a European way station than deepest Morocco.

One Sunday still early in the fall, as I mentioned, we took the train to El Escorial, Felipe the Second's massive funereal baroque palace, and then marched up a long hill to the kitschy cavernous fascist monument to the Spanish Civil War, called Valle de los Caídos or "Valley of the Fallen." On our walk back to the train station we had a discussion that quickly became an argument about Existentialism, the philosophy of the day, later debunked to a lower order. Influenced by my brother-in-law, who admired and was always reading Camus on his weekends in Fire Island, I defended Existentialism. Curt was not so convinced and played the Devil's avocado (punster Cabrera Infante's bilingual quip). Probably the exhausting hike, if not the oppressive kitsch of that monstrous fascist monument, was responsible for this foolish argument.

At the university, every day after morning classes, we would all partake of the cheery Spanish ritual of gathering at nearby bars for an aperitif before *el almuerzo*, which was often a three-course meal sometimes including a magnificent paella. With Spanish men or mostly boys I was learning slang, like the word "cojonudo" which to me sounded like lame (cojo) knot (nudo) and therefore made no sense. I was quickly enlightened by the ensuing laughter that I was off track and learned from some *madrileño* that this superlative adjective derived from the word "cojones," meaning testicles, an emphatic or crude way of saying "Awesome!" Hyperbole, I quickly learned, was the cornerstone of Spanish discourse.

Within the exotic was the familiar: sometimes closing my eyes, in the funky part of Madrid where I lived, just above the dry Manzanares River, almost on the outskirts, I was so nostalgic for home that at times I could feel I was back in Washington Heights, that tree-lined outskirt of northern Manhattan and melting pot of European refugees during my childhood. Speaking of refugees, many centuries ago in Spain, Arabs and Jews had been a vital presence, and it was inevitable that many Catholics in the present-day country were *conversos*, from Jewish families that had converted, a choice given to them at the time of the Inquisition, when the other choices were either death by torture or exile. I thought about this during that year, seeing faces in the city that could easily have descended from those *conversos*.

I fell easily into Spanish, like a shoe that fit, as if some part of me came out in the performance of the language. All language is performative, as the philosopher J.L. Austin taught, and to mimic this language of superlatives seemed to require one to speak more assertively or confidently or maybe just louder than in American English. Spanish is such a flexible language with its diminutives and augmentatives, expressive usages we don't have in English. Jokes and wordplays expanded my repertoire exponentially during that year. Thanks to "immersion," the basic strategy of Education Abroad language programs, I became fluent as did many if not all of my American comrades in Madrid, where I spent my junior year of college, an escape from the ivory tower of Vassar College.

The saying goes that the pillow is the best teacher of any language, and this is a truism that I and many can confirm. But even just going out with Spanish friends to enjoy bustling bars with their animated bartenders, where tapas were always served with beer or wine, expanded our vocabularies and maybe even our waistlines. Some bars had the delightful custom of permitting customers to drop soiled little napkins or olive pits on the floor and periodically a floor sweeper would come by with an ample broom to clear away the debris under our feet. We got to know which bar specialized in which tapa, for example, miniature "Moorish" meat brochettes called "pinchos morunos" or olives stuffed with anchovies, or grilled prawns or Spanish tortillas. It was the jolly custom to stop for an espresso or a *tinto* and socialize after morning classes at the university. The long afternoons and evenings, as the high plateau sun set, were especially pleasurable, a time of day called "la tarde." Curiously the word "tarde" which as an adjective means late, as a noun means both afternoon and evening, one of many conundrums when translating into English. Madrid was (and still is) a city that came to life especially at night, buzzing with activity until the wee hours of the morning, and so, in a way, our university was also those lively nights wandering from tapa to tapa.

Coming home late on those extended leisurely nights of Madrid meant clapping hands for the *sereno*—the night watchman—and hoping he was nearby, to open the door to the building where you lived. The word "sereno" was like poetry, a metonym for the thing itself, as if the watchman's main function was to preserve the night's serenity merely by being there. Often, you'd have to find your way in total darkness on the indoor stairs because the "one-minute light" sometimes didn't even last a minute and didn't give you enough time to reach the next button before the minute was up. Then you were on your own and had to find the next button, groping along the walls in the dark, and run up step by step before the light went out again.

The Señora discouraged late nights, but I think this was so that we wouldn't disturb her or Alicia's sleep—or was this a show of concern for our safety? What remains in memory, what I am trying earnestly to bring back to life, is ultimately tenuous, dreamlike, a magical trace of nights roaming the Cava Baja or festive fairs like the Night of San Juan along the river, with José, Ramon or Miguel or some other long forgotten boyfriend. Or afternoons with their long shadows, walking along the narrow, evocative cobble-stoned streets, heading to a bookstore or library or to a date at a café in a picturesque square, places that became so familiar and are now so far away in the mist of time.

3

1968: Emir and Latin Literary Life

My first year at Columbia University ended with the May '68 protest riots and sit-downs against the war in Vietnam, also intense meetings in the upper westside smoke-filled pads of "revolutionaries" or student leaders, which I attended with boyfriends who felt committed to the protests. The daughter of a civil servant who had liked Ike, and who was a second-generation American, I resisted hating the country that was home and had been a refuge to our persecuted ancestors; of course, I felt like everyone around me that this war, like all wars, was horrendous, especially because our role in it was unjustified—a realization that now seems abundantly clear. But I could not embrace slogans wholeheartedly, and I believe, more than anything, I was fixed upon survival, or worried about where my life was going.

Like Scarlett O'Hara caught blindly in her own dramas amid the horrors of the Civil War, I felt my own private struggles were difficult enough for me to handle at twenty-one. Her refrain, "What's to become of me?"—a lament not only ironic but also iconic in the history of womanhood—was a thought very much on my mind in those years. The war, like the world, belonged to men after all, which included the scruffy long-haired male students getting high on pot and mimicking their radical heroes. Weren't their fierce protests an expression of machismo as well as a struggle against authority? Nonetheless, as the Sixties became the Seventies, my consciousness was raised, especially around sexual politics, its impact on every individual, on the arts and every aspect of life, especially on the lives and rights of women. The new sexual freedom of the 1960s, while it was a progressive trend, was just a beginning. In a way the feminist movement served to liberate men (this was Manuel Puig's central idea in *Kiss of the Spider Woman*) so that, at least, they could understand or respond with better understanding to the dilemmas of women.

Before finding an apartment myself and two roommates could afford, I lived that first summer, 1967, the Summer of Love, in "International House" overlooking Riverside Drive. Off the university campus, this beehive was a kind of co-ed transition from dormitory life to real life. Many well-known intellectuals, Philip Roth for example, had lived in that multi-national, multi-ethnic apiary as students. Flirting was the one thing we all could afford and what we certainly had in common. Amid the swarm of young men, I encountered in International House was a sensual Brahmin from Calcutta, with exquisite features, a South African (or rather Rhodesian) Brit, Gil Cottrell, who became a very kindly boyfriend for a while, and then there was Sadik, a tall dark attractive Turkish guy.

I had a crush on Sadik, who never failed to pontificate whenever he had an audience of a group of us or even only myself. We all would often meet at breakfast in the mess hall, and sexy Sadik had the conviction that he knew everything and was the wisest man in the world. His mostly female followers, including me, believed with utter naivete every word he uttered. One flaw during much of my life has been to accept the authority of men who appear intelligent. That flaw has diminished, thankfully with the years and my own accomplishments. The oddest thing is that we, the followers of Sadik, never found out if he was even really a student, or even if he were Turkish? Such are the follies of youth. Not totally, as after that summer I came to the realization, thanks to a conversation with an ex-Vassar girl named Lynn who was going to be one of my roommates, that our Turkish dilettante was most probably a bullshit artist.

The bustling Columbia campus with its broad promenade between majestic buildings, and its westside neighborhood from 110th to 120th street, from Riverside Drive to Amsterdam Avenue, was buzzing not only with scholarly ambitions but with the free-floating eros of the hippie era. This was a time of self-realization and misadventures, I even dated businessmen and, I believe, once or twice, gangsters. One of those fellows whose name I don't recall took me out in his Jaguar convertible to the Playboy club, a novelty at that time which had cachet. The half-asleep feminist in me evidently reacted, as I never again darkened the threshold of that despicable den where waitresses had to wear tight bunny suits with a cotton ball on their butt.

To have enough money to live as a graduate student—a kind of oxymoron really—I had applied to the federal work-study program and got a job that promised to be interesting at the local radio station. WRVR was a serious institution that featured interviews of important cultural figures and classical music as well as jazz, housed on the top floor of the Riverside Church tower on 122nd Street and Riverside Drive. As an intern I was in the company of clever men—studio technicians and fellow work-study Columbia students—and it felt comfortable to be the only girl among these fellow workers.

The director of the radio station, Mr. Summerfield, whose first name I can't remember, had a certain *savoir faire*, a mischievous glint in his eye. He or I or all of us came up at one of our first meetings with the idea of running a two-hour weekly rock show: the initial inspiration came from a guest to the station, the writer Richard Kostelanetz who was interviewed on the new rock music of the 1960s. Like some of those girls at Vassar College who went after their professors, I was drawn to older men, mostly conditioned by the Hollywood movies and my early crushes on the likes of Cary Grant and especially Gregory Peck (though both were unique specimens). While such attractions seemed physical, as I matured, I realized the main appeal was something else, that men, as opposed to boys, had power, and I seemed to need protection or guidance.

Older men were appealing because they seemed more confident, and I was a child who had grown up accustomed to being with older people much more than with my own generation. It is hard for me to relate to these feelings now, and I can barely remember how I felt then. Mr. Summerfield was married like most middle-aged men those days, but sexual freedom in the Sixties gave married men more permission than ever. Our dalliance was channeled, fortunately, into work: I and the other work-study students were there to assist the programming as well as to learn. Encouraged by the friendly casual atmosphere of the station and my fellow interns, I proposed a program featuring the baroque concerto. Thanks to the excellent music history course I had taken senior year at Vassar, crowned by a class excursion to the Met at Lincoln Center, I put together the program notes.

Encouraged by the lively yet laid back ambience of the radio station, I had the gumption to accept Mr. Summerfield's invitation to emcee a rock program, a first (and probably last) at WRVR Riverside Church Radio. As it was still a novelty in the 1960s to have a female disk jockey—the only one in New York then was Alison Steele, whose *nom de guerre* was "The Nightbird"—Summerfield had proposed enthusiastically, "Jill has to do it!"; that I run the show, to be called "Just Rock with Just Jill" as a follow-up to RVR's excellent "Just Jazz" program with Ed Beach, very popular among aficionados like my brother-in-law. An elegant bohemian with a deep voice and mustache, Ed was a hard act to follow, but he tried to give me some pointers. At that time, I was still entertaining a vague career plan that involved music, to put, somehow, my musical training to "practical" use.

"Just Rock" was a two-hour Friday evening show—repeated Saturday afternoons—which even had fans and lasted over a year. WRVR's main virtue

Figure 3.1 Jill at WRVR, New York City, 1967–68. (Photo credit: Trude Fleischmann.)

was the total lack of invasive commercials, and so, unlike other pop music stations, would allow for the novelty of a commercial-free flow of the latest greatest rock music from Frank Zappa to Mama Cass. I enjoyed the actual programming much more than speaking to an invisible audience, and often designed theme programs, or focused on an instrument, such as a whole program segment highlighting keyboard performances.

Beatlemania still ran high and 1967–68 were big years for rock and soul. The segment I particularly relished putting together was "Sunshine and Satire" bringing The Lovin' Spoonful and the Beach Boys together with the Mothers of Invention and the Rolling Stones. We all loved the clever lyrics and absurd humor of the "Mothers" and some of their suggestive "inventions" remain with me, like "Walking through the prunes, in June ..." Many songs we played were or would become classics, from the latest Beatles and Stones to the exciting pulse of

Motown, Stevie Wonder, Otis Redding, Martha and the Vandellas, and Marvin Gaye, to the West coast Beach Boys and the Doors who lit our fire. "Just Rock" featured them all and the list goes on: Simon and Garfunkel, Dylan, Country Joe and the Fish, the Rascals, the Jefferson Airplane, Procol Harum, and the one and only Aretha Franklin and her R-E-S-P-E-C-T.

As the months wore on, despite my taciturn hosting style, I even received the occasional fan mail (sparse compared to the barrage that Ed Beach received), but I was shy about public speaking and so, despite the encouraging atmosphere, remained an often silent disk jockey. The most I said to introduce each show, speaking into the mike, was "This is Just Rock with Just Jill, and today's show will feature …" Not exactly a river of clever chatter, but I learned to work the turntable at least.

In the spring semester in 1968, shortly before my job at the radio station ended, I was taking Gregory Rabassa's class on the Latin American novel in the old Hispanic House at Columbia University, located at the genteel end of Claremont Avenue—a mere five or six blocks south of 125th Street, very close to where I still lived. Friendly and yet reserved, often with an impish grin on his lively face, Rabassa was already eminent in the New York literary world, having won in 1964 the first National Book Award to honor a translator, for his first major publication, Julio Cortázar's masterpiece *Hopscotch*, the labyrinthine odyssey of an exiled Argentine writer in Paris which was also a contrived, infinite puzzle with set pieces that were grand moments of absurd comedy. The gifted Greg had rendered this Joycean tour de force with masterful panache.

One complex novel we read that caught my attention was about a disillusioned modern man who vanishes into the jungle seeking new and special music he has heard that could be found in a primitive, sensual world. Titled "The Lost Steps" (*Los pasos perdidos*), this romantic or rather utopic adventure was the work of a prominent Cuban writer, Alejo Carpentier, who was also a great scholar of Cuban music as well as the Revolution's cultural attaché in Paris. Ten years after I took his class—and after translating literary works from Argentina and Cuba such as *Betrayed by Rita Hayworth*, *Heartbreak Tango* and *Three Trapped Tigers*, perchance more innovative and untranslatable than *Hopscotch*—I would be invited to join Greg on the same jury along with television personality Kitty Carlyle to select the recipient of the 1978 National Book Award in Translation.

But that was the future in the present, which was 1968 when Gregory Rabassa, mild-mannered yet legendary translator, inadvertently set me on a path.

Figure 3.2 Jill and Greg Rabassa, National Book Awards, New York City, 1978. (Photo credit: Martha Holmes.)

Inadvertently, because Greg was not my appointed mentor, nor did I study with him except for that one course. Greg, as his students and friends would tell you, was an amiable soft-spoken man whose features vaguely recalled the spaghetti western bad cowboy Lee Van Cleef. He was not a rigorous professor but with his distinct tone and voice, Greg, born in Vermont and the son of a Cuban father, was an irrepressible storyteller with an ironic folksy style. One afternoon after class, I dared to approach his desk to ask him, "How does one start translating?" A question that generations of students, in turn, have asked me.

Greg advised me with his plain-spoken candor that "The way to start translating is to translate," and he suggested I pay a visit to a newly founded institute called the Center of Inter-American Relations—previously home to the Russian embassy—located at 680 Park Avenue. Once there, I should introduce myself to the literature program director, José Guillermo Castillo. So, in March or April, I made my way downtown from Columbia University, via subway and crosstown bus, to the elegant east side address on Park Avenue and 68th Street. I didn't know what to expect while waiting in the neo-classic entrance hall. I was pleasantly surprised when Castillo, who was also a Venezuelan artist, stepped out of the elevator to greet me. In his smart pin-striped suit, he had the face of a mischievous cherub and welcomed me with a relaxed Caribbean informality.

We stood chatting in the lobby because, he explained, workers were still in the process of setting up the Center. He told me his goal was to promote the arts of Latin America in general but very specifically to support translations of the great and, especially, new Latin American writers. I informed him that I would be spending the summer on an exchange program in Cali, Colombia. I had chosen Colombia for my own reasons: Curt was in the Peace Corps there. (It was reassuring to go to a country where I had a friend, but I foolishly fantasized we might resume the relationship we had nipped in the bud, and despite intimate moments with him that summer, the bud would remain nipped.)

José Guillermo Castillo enthusiastically urged me to bring back books or plays by new writers whom I might discover there. He even advised me, before leaving New York, to consult Joanne Pottlitzer, a playwright acquaintance of his who founded and directed New York City's TOLA, Theater of Latin America. Joanne was also very approachable and mentioned a few names of writers I could seek out. And so, aside from the exchange program job I would have in a factory in Cali, I now had a mission. Thanks to Joanne's suggestions, I visited the "Experimental Theater" of Cali, where I would meet its founder, the playwright Enrique Buenaventura, whose last name, the name of a city in Colombia, meant, fortuitously, "good fortune." Connecting with this playwright was a kind of rehearsal, because when I returned to visit José Castillo that September with a brief translation sample of one of Buenaventura's plays, the director had another plan for me.

It's a miracle (I now think) that I got safely back to New York at the end of that August. Disembarking from the Bogota flight at the airport now called JFK, I went through Customs with an illicit stash of Colombian Gold. A new boyfriend, a New Yorker with a nice mustache named Joe Wolf who, like Curt, was in the Peace Corps in Colombia, had sent me back with this dangerous cargo. Waiting for me at JFK was yet another boyfriend named Joe who had indeed requested that I bring back "gold" which I could hide cleverly, he instructed me, inside the covers of a carved-out book. Shortly before, departing from Bogota, I remember a pleasurable high, one sunset in a park with Joe (the mustache) and I sitting under a tall palm tree whose branches slowly swayed like a giant leisurely spider suspended languorously above us. At Customs, surrounded by officers of the law with a supply of aromatic marijuana in my luggage, I managed to re-enter the country unscathed.

*

Back in the big city, I was more anxious than ever for some gear to catch, for some clear sense of direction. I thought writing could help me, and continued filling small notebooks with diary scribbles that often went from noting the virtues versus limitations of a new boyfriend to expressing (with naivete) existential angst. My diary in Spain had some interest but mainly registered places visited or presented bits of an "I" seen through a fog of laments about the meaning of life. I read a lot, traveling to foreign worlds with gurus like Malcolm Lowry, Herman Hesse, Mishima, Lawrence Durrell. Upon reading Durrell, I longed to travel to Egypt and to be in the decadent world of the mysterious Justine. (I still haven't been to Egypt, alas.) But even more I wanted to be the writers I was reading, like Virginia Woolf or Donald Barthelme, creative artists, each in her or his generation, of English prose. José Guillermo Castillo, the affable director of the CIAR Literature Program—nowadays he might be pegged a smooth operator—invited me to be a research assistant for the Center. My research credentials as a graduate student at Columbia University were sufficient; I would be working with a trio of distinguished scholars headed by Monegal, a newly appointed Yale professor, and including my professor Greg Rabassa to produce the first annotated compendium of Latin American literary works translated into English. The third member of the bibliography committee was a younger professor and critic, John Alexander Coleman, who taught at NYU. A flamboyant Irish American (whose father had once been the mayor of Hartford) John was a jazz and classical music maven as well as a seasoned Hispanist who had received his doctoral degree at Harvard and had also studied in Spain. Like the Princeton-trained Alfred MacAdam whom I later met in New Haven, John spoke amazingly perfect Spanish for a gringo; both these impressive younger professors were equally versed in Portuguese.

As time would tell, John Coleman and Greg Rabassa with their university duties were probably more enthusiastic about the "business" lunches than about the bibliography itself. Our favorite Chinese restaurant for these meetings was two blocks east of the Center, on 68th Street and 3rd Avenue, and José Guillermo was the generous host.

This was an era when to be an attractive young woman was both an advantage and a disadvantage. With my look of a French ingenue in a 1960s Godard film with straight bangs and miniskirt, my presence as "assistant" perhaps made these lunches even more appealing to the men. However, when Emir was first apprised of my participation, that is, before we met, he remarked (according to José Guillermo Castillo), "What's a young girl supposed to be doing here?" I am sure that had I been a male graduate student, both the appeal and the disapproval would have been absent. The much-discussed bibliography would never be completed, partly because of insufficient funding and because Emir Rodríguez Monegal was the only seriously motivated member of the committee.

Emir was born in Melo, a small town on the Brazilian border of Uruguay, that tiny nation squeezed between Argentina and Brazil, but his mother and he soon moved to the capital, Montevideo, while his father (who he would learn was a stepfather) was away at work in the Brazilian jungle. Without his real father, Emir had a challenging childhood but fortunately had affectionate aunts and uncles on his mother's side. During Emir's youth, Uruguay had been labeled the Switzerland of Latin America for its agrarian reforms, economic progress, social welfare programs and a high literacy rate, and mainly because it wasn't a Catholic country like most of South America.

An avid reader and student at the Lycée Française in Montevideo, at the age of fifteen, Emir had encountered the literary passion of his life, browsing through *El Hogar* ("Home"), a women's magazine on his mother's night table. Here he found and followed a weekly series of remarkable miniature biographies of important world writers like Virginia Woolf and William Faulkner. The author of these astounding pieces in the 1930s was none other than an obscure Argentine writer named Jorge Luis Borges.

Years later, Emir would be a critic closely associated with the so-called Latin American Boom in the same way that Edmund "Bunny" Wilson had been the crucial advocate, with seminal critical works such as Axel's *Castle*, of the major literary figures of Anglo modernism. Often called simply Monegal—a resonant name sounding like "my equal" in French—Emir spread the word about key writers with his literary biographies, a genre less practiced in Spanish than in English or French, and he wrote the first biography of Borges in English, published by E.P. Dutton, the same press that issued Borges's works in the 1970s. Emir Rodríguez Monegal had the dubious honor of being among Borges's acquaintances and friends who were transformed into fiction, as in the gaucho story called "La otra muerte" ("The Other Death").

To celebrate the brand-new literature program, the bibliography committee met on October 22, the day after my twenty-second birthday, for what was my first business luncheon—although my last year in high school, I had attended a formal luncheon at the exclusive wood-paneled Oak Room in the Plaza Hotel, in an era when women were not allowed to dine there. Celebrating our farewell as editors of the high school newspaper *Overtone* as well as our imminent graduation, this prestigious moment was a major event for me and my schoolmates.

Having returned from Colombia at the beginning of September 1968, I looked forward to the gathering hosted by José Guillermo Castillo, as a significant step into professional life. I already knew Greg and had met John Coleman at the Center on a previous occasion. That autumnal sunny Sunday, October 22, 1968, I took the subway uptown to Rockefeller Center and walked briskly in the crisp cold air to 666 Sixth Avenue, where José Guillermo had reserved a table at a restaurant on the top floor. This vertiginous location pertained to a swanky Szechuan Chinese restaurant. The only kind of Chinese restaurants I (and most Americans) knew up until then were Cantonese. Chinese and Cantonese were synonymous in my childhood, and the usual fare of egg rolls, spareribs, egg drop soup and chicken chow mein was a festive "exotic" outing.

I was the first to arrive that fateful Sunday, wearing a wool coat, silk blouse, a new suede miniskirt, and high leather boots: this was the era of Twiggy and swinging London made mini-skirts de rigueur. The elevator took me all the way up to the penthouse and I was greeted at the entrance by the ceremonious Chinese maître d' who invited me to sit in the waiting lounge. I didn't wait for long. A tall portly Latin-looking gentleman with an umbrella on his arm, formally attired in a dark suit and sober tie under his overcoat, briskly entered and asked for our party. He glanced at me as he removed his overcoat, and I felt encouraged to approach: "You must be Emir Rodríguez Monegal."

He smiled, shook my hand, and with this introduction to each other I felt reassured, more at ease now that I knew all the committee members. There was an electricity in Monegal's presence, a great vitality. At the same time, he appeared so dignified, from another era almost, in part because of his somber suit and bearing. You could almost see him in the role of Emil Jannings, the "Herr Professor" in Marlene Dietrich's film made in Germany which made her famous, when the eccentric provincial professor shows up at the "Blue Angel" nightclub to protect his students from debauchery and ends up being seduced by the blonde cabaret singer. In his dark suit, white shirt, and tie, with raven black hair, long face with intense dark eyes and thick dark eyebrows, Emir also had a touch of the sinister à la Bela Lugosi's Dracula. In brief, he looked European (as did many Latin Americans) in contrast with the casual North American academic look. The note of irony in his face, a kind of amused confidence, was a charming part of this worldly picture, and there was a warmth about him too.

The others showed up soon after: José Guillermo, his pretty wife Ana Maria, and Greg Rabassa who, with his quiet charm and humor, launched (I believe) into one of his folksy Vermont stories after we were seated at an ample round table. The last to arrive was the buoyant John Alexander Coleman, who I had met once before in José's office and who was wearing bright pastel colors—I believe a light blue jacket and very yellow tie and possibly checkered trousers. John always would dress in his own eccentric mode: was it a preppy look or an insouciant statement? He swept in with his frequent hearty greeting—"maestro!"—to Emir, then Greg, and shaking hands with all. John and Emir knew each other already, though this might have been only the second or third time they had met in person.

I can't remember how much or if we talked at all about the project, but the savory and spicy dishes on the lazy Susan in the center of the table, and the polite service were all superb, accompanied by an uninterrupted flow of cocktails and Chinese tea. The conversation was animated, anecdotes and the latest literary or political gossip flying back and forth across the table, and I added my two cents at some point, managing to keep up with the jokes in Spanish. With its cheerful energy, this occasion, my first real business lunch as it were, was a big deal for a mere graduate student. Every person around the table was older and so accomplished except for Ana Maria, but still, the event had a happily familiar feel. After all, I had grown up in a family where I was used to being the only child surrounded by loquacious adults.

After lunch came to an end with its panoply of fortune cookies, Emir pulled me aside to say: "I am meeting some friends, why don't you join us?" and we went down the elevator together. In the main lobby he was greeted by two elegant women. The more statuesque lady was a middle-aged blonde Emir proudly introduced as the "great Uruguayan actress China Zorrilla" who energetically embraced him and cast me a charming smile, as did Elizabeth Fonseca, the petite and alluring wife of a distinguished Uruguayan sculptor and architect, Gonzalo Fonseca. I walked them to the curb where they piled into a taxi that Emir had hailed, heading downtown. Knowing that I was heading that way too, Emir insisted I join them in the now jam-packed cab so, ignoring the grumbling driver, we barreled down Fifth Avenue.

China (pronounced Cheena), the *rioplatense* nickname for her indisputably Catholic name, Concepción, was amusingly overbearing and spoke English with what could be described as a British Uruguayan accent. Emir would later explain to me when we were alone, that the Spanish nickname Concha could not be used in Uruguay and Argentina because it (literally meaning seashell) was slang for vagina, hence the use of China as the short form of Concepción. (The dictionary meaning of "China" in Spanish is Chinese female, but in Argentina it can also mean lower-class girl or from a racially mixed background.) Elizabeth, perky, deep-voiced and petite, was flirting with Emir. I had a vague sense that Elizabeth Fonseca and her sculptor/architect husband Gonzalo, glamorous fauna of the West Village, had an open marriage. In any case, Emir and friends were off to a party at the Fonseca's townhouse on West 11th Street, and I returned to my modest studio apartment in a six-story red brick building on the corner of Waverly and Tenth.

After the Chinese restaurant event, Emir and I ran into each other at the Center once or twice again in the following weeks; we were starting work on the bibliography which meant occasional visits to the convenient xerox machine on the fourth floor, near a water cooler. On those occasions I noticed him noticing me, usually in my ubiquitous suede miniskirt and I sensed, absurdly despite the age difference, that I was beginning to feel attracted to this exotic gentleman. He would come into the city on Thursdays or Fridays from New Haven where he was still visiting professor and about to be the appointed chair of the Spanish and Portuguese Department.

Emir had published, as mentioned, one of the first substantial essays on García Márquez's novel, entitled "Anachronisms and Novelty in *One Hundred Years of Solitude*."[2] This critical study revealed eye-opening connections between the novel and García Márquez's readings of Faulkner and Virginia Woolf as well as *Pedro Páramo*, the most significant novel, or novella, about the era of the Mexican Revolution. These ideas and the initial research for the Latin American bibliography would both help me develop my M.A. thesis on the "genesis" of *One Hundred Years of Solitude* and how García Márquez's novel cleverly interfaced diverse and significant literary influences.

We made a date to have lunch together in November, a week or two before Thanksgiving. I was to meet Emir in the lobby of the hotel where he was staying in the city, the Biltmore Commodore, then perched conveniently above Grand Central Station, where he would arrive, directly from New Haven. It was a Friday around noon and people were bustling everywhere, checking out or just loitering. I was a little nervous about this "date." Was it wise to open the door (as it were) to anything other than a professional relationship with this man?

The huge lobby was hectic and noisy, which somehow made me agitated. Instead of waiting downstairs, where it was crowded and there was nowhere to sit, I impulsively followed people into an elevator. Had he given me the room number, or had they given it to me at the desk? I don't remember but I do remember that I went directly to his floor and room and knocked on the door. Having just checked in himself, he quickly opened with a look of surprise, saying "Oh! you're here—well, come in."

We didn't stay in his room for more than a few minutes. First, he immediately announced that he had had a busy week of classes at Yale, and then "I won't be a moment, please sit down" while he opened a closet door and took out his coat. I sat down in an armchair he indicated, near the entrance of the room. I think he was a little taken aback that I had come upstairs instead of waiting in the lobby. I felt slightly embarrassed about the intimate situation which my arrival had abruptly created. I don't recall what we were talking about next, but suddenly he was kneeling beside me, and saying, softly, "You have the most beautiful skin."

Sitting apprehensively in the ample armchair facing the door I had entered, I recall that, at that moment, I was feeling an impulse to spring out of the room. His dark friendly eyes were smiling and looking into my eyes. The attraction I also felt seemed so incongruous: a forbidden older man, imposing, with dark prominent eyebrows, a long Spanish face, and his thick straight black hair slicked back. He was a big man (as I noted before) and with his name which in Arabic means "leader," Emir could have passed for Valentino's *Sheik of Araby*, though not in sheik's clothing.

I was struck again by the powerful effect, almost like a thunderbolt, I was having on this exceptionally articulate man, who with his slight Latin accent tinged with British English again repeated, as if he couldn't find other words, "I have never seen such beautiful skin so close; I've never seen such beautiful skin." I don't remember what was said next, but we both rose quickly. Emir put on his coat—I was still wearing mine—and we left the perilous hotel room to go to lunch.

On the elevator down to the lobby, we discussed where we should have lunch. In the lobby once again and feeling embarrassed with this older man, as if everyone's eyes were upon us which I am sure wasn't the case, I quickly suggested a popular restaurant downtown in Greenwich Village: La Trattoria on the triangular corner where 6th Avenue and 4th St. meet Cornelia St. It had turned into a surprisingly sunny day for November, and so we agreed it would be nice to walk for a while. To me this also felt safer. I couldn't figure out what he was thinking except that he was happy to be with me. Our walk became a leisurely hike from midtown to the Village.

I was still worried about how startling it had been for him to see such a young face suddenly so close to his, and so I was not quite over the embarrassment of showing up at Emir's room. It was something that seemed natural to me then, and would have been, if I had been getting together with a relative or with a friend my age. But, in this case, it could easily be interpreted as an advance that I wasn't sure I intended.

We, or at least I, ordered linguini in clam sauce, a detail I remember as *vongole* has always been a favorite dish. We both ordered wine, which neither of us usually had at midday. In our conversation that day, each of us felt free to speak of our respective personal lives and history, and this was when I learned of his imminent divorce from a Uruguayan society woman named Magdalena. This divorce would be finalized in 1971, and I would learn from him that it was stressful for both parties, as well as for his two children in their upper teens from an earlier marriage, and especially for his toddler son Alejandro, his child with Magdalena.

Aside from our shared enthusiasm over *One Hundred Years of Solitude*, other topics during that first intimate conversation ranged from the French New Wave cinema to "relationships." I spoke of my interactions with young men my age and about my family, my being the "kid sister" in the family. He gathered an impression of my reluctance to leave childhood behind, because of my environment as a child surrounded by preoccupied adults. Being a real woman, like my eldest sister Alice, meant heavy responsibilities with kids and meant being compliant with aggressive men like my brother-in-law. It seemed as if becoming a woman was associated with the acceptance of death or maybe my mother's sudden, early death left me with this harsh message, a cruel irony to grow into womanhood at the very moment my beautiful mother was dying.

As a pre-pubescent teenager, my curiosity about sex had been discouraged by my old-fashioned mother who, when I dared to tell her a boy had kissed or touched me, was not pleased and made it clear that I should stay away, it was "dirty." By the time my sisters tried to help me with carnal knowledge, I was worried about prohibitions including a fear of pregnancy out of wedlock, a very common fear in those days before Roe vs Wade—a sadly ironic observation in current history. And the forceful attitudes of men and boys were mostly off-putting.

These explanations or complaints gave Emir the cue to compare the Latin lover with the American man who, according to him, was mainly interested in fellatio. I couldn't argue the point. He vigorously criticized American men, which was somehow music to my ears, because it justified what I rejected. Then he walked me home. Maybe it was the wine, as I invited him up to my place. In the elevator I again regretted my reckless invitation, also as we entered my studio apartment. According to him, this was the first time he was seriously attracted to a much younger woman. He was forty-seven and I was twenty-two, but I sure looked or seemed much younger.

The door opened onto a kitchenette with a little French café-style table and then one stepped through a clattering curtain of wooden beads—a hippie touch left by the previous tenant. I had a comfortable single bed that would be replaced a few months later with a less comfortable convertible sofa bed. In this confined space my desk and bookshelves were placed against the opposite wall. The only two windows faced an airshaft, and between them a KLH stereo set generously given to me by my brother-in-law, Alice's husband.

Emir sat down and asked me to sit on his lap.

"You know, I'm not that naïve" or "Yo no soy tan naïve," I said in Spanglish (as the word "ingenua" for naïve was not yet in my vocabulary or simply, I couldn't call it up) after hesitantly accepting his invitation, using the subject pronoun for unnecessary emphasis: In Spanish the subject pronoun is normally omitted except for clarification as well as emphasis, so my use of "yo" on that occasion was a gringa touch. This first intimacy, as I now look back from a comfortable distant, seems like Proust's staging of Swann's first moment alone with Odette in the carriage, the moment in which a passion surreptitiously blossomed. "Well, there's nothing to be afraid of—I just want to count the beauty marks on your neck," Emir said with a warm voice and slightly ironic smile as he looked into my eyes, and, with his glasses on, then examined carefully, almost painstakingly, each little spot as if he were a doctor scanning the body of a bashful patient, which is how I felt, fearful of an imminent invasion.

We moved, almost imperceptibly, over to my single bed but with the single purpose of continuing to count beauty marks, or moles as they are called less coyly. I think we came up with twenty-two, a fearful symmetry. I believe he kissed me gently on the neck, then I am sure my anxiety reached its limit, and I led him to the door. *Progrès en amour assez lents*, as a Frenchman would write, a book I later received from Argentine writer Bioy Casares. Emir and I finally crossed the threshold in his apartment in New Haven. Though I had already lost my virginity, somehow with him it was like the first time. I had a definite propensity for older men but the problem with Emir as a serious fiancé was not only was he twenty-five years older but that he looked like he could be my father.

In restaurants, in public, at a party or a gathering outside of Emir's academic world, I sometimes felt embarrassed, convinced that people looked upon us as an odd couple. A little like Audrey Hepburn and Gary Cooper in *Love in the Afternoon* though without the Hollywood glamour. Gary Cooper seemed so much older, enough to be the exquisite young actress's father, that, like Emir and myself, the romance between those two seemed incongruous.

In my case Emir was replacing not only father but also mother. He was a man of firm convictions but also was caring and protective, and he helped me to believe in myself and in the scholarly career for which I was headed. Emir and I looked to everyone like father and daughter, or, as Manuel Puig later euphemistically put it, a "striking" couple. Emir heard this amusing comment from a mutual friend that Manuel's first impression was that we were "una pareja llamativa" which could also mean an "odd" couple. "Llamativa" was basically a campy euphemism, typical of the speech of Puig's mother, Malé, and her generation. It literally means something that calls attention to itself.

When on our trip to Rio de Janeiro and Buenos Aires in 1971, Emir and I visited Manuel at his parent's home, I realized that his mother was the source of those local voices Manuel reproduced so meticulously in his novels. The adventure of translating his writing lay in those spoken Argentine clichés and phrases that had to find their tone in English. Hearing her speak was so uncanny that at times I couldn't contain a giggle of recognition, which puzzled Malé who then queried Manuel, and he flatly explained: "You sound like my novel." In the years that followed Manuel visited us often in New Haven, indeed his friendship with Emir became closer when I was living with Emir. I think this was largely because Manuel felt more comfortable with girlfriends, hence my presence eased them into a more informal dialogue.

An eclectic reader as well as a dedicated literary scholar, Emir knew more about movies than anyone I knew before I met Cabrera Infante and Puig, and had an extraordinary sensibility. Though I already had dalliances or attachments with bright young men and a few poets like the craggy Canadian Mark Strand, Emir seemed to get me in a way no other male person had. He felt like salvation from the downwardly mobile hippiedom of my contemporaries, and the warm embrace of a world richer than the New York literary scene.

José Guillermo had introduced me to Mark Strand upon my return from Colombia, so that I could assist him as Spanish "informant," to help him translate an impressive range of modern and contemporary Mexican poets, like Salvador Novo and Tomas Segovia, in an important anthology that Octavio Paz had just edited. This collaboration, which taught Mark some Spanish (which he finished learning on his visits to Octavio and his sexy wife Marie Jo) and gave me lessons in poetry, was a prelude to my translation career which truly began with Emir.

Translation, even when you do it totally alone, is always a collaboration with the shadowy author. I have since discovered that this was a common occurrence to other translators who (male as well as female) like my dear departed friend Carol Maier, had acquired carnal knowledge in the process of working with a Cuban poet with whom there was, inevitably, a mutual attraction.

The years with Emir were incredibly productive and we led a disciplined life as do many writers, every morning devoted to writing or translation. Emir was writing his biography of Jorge Luis Borges for E.P. Dutton while I was plodding through my first translations. Emir helped me revise them until the year before he died, page by patient page, and, in turn, I would revise his English as this was the first time, and I believe the only occasion, that he wrote an entire book in English. Here was a prodigious literary critic, the author of many books and hundreds of articles, who had an encyclopedic breadth of knowledge about the arts and especially the cinema, whose first film review at the age of twenty, in 1941, was of *Citizen Kane*.

While literary work filled our life together, the movies were our shared addiction. From expressionism to the new wave, from Lubitsch to Fritz Lang, from Howard Hawks to Claude Chabrol, from Alfred Hitchcock to Godard, Fellini, Rohmer and Truffaut, the late 1960s and 1970s was an eye-opening era of auteur directors and new ones that kept emerging, but also a time when the Hollywood classics began to be studied seriously. The first film Emir and I saw together in a theater in Manhattan was Ingmar Bergman's *Skamen* or "Shame"— not a lightweight! This morose black-and-white Swedish film was about Vietnam and the legacy of the Second World War, and ultimately about the effect of war on the relationship of a couple, musicians living on a remote island farm, played by Max Von Sydow and the young Liv Ullman. At dinner afterwards in one of those traditional steak houses in midtown, we had our first of many animated conversations about a movie or play we experienced together.

Emir's earliest book was about the new film director Ingmar Bergman, co-written with his fellow Uruguayan film critic and journalist, Homero Alsina Thevenet, a slight, poker-faced and kinetic man who looked a little like Charlie Chaplin and did uncanny imitations of Groucho Marx in perfectly nuanced English. Homero was perhaps Emir's closest friend who I met on that unforgettable trip to Buenos Aires, and who I would later see again in Spain and also when I visited lovely Montevideo.

Bergman was a major innovator in those days, especially since he was among the most serious filmmakers to place sex and psychological problems in the foreground, and our conversations were filled with films and actors like the magnificent Von Sydow or those iconic beautiful Bergman women like Liv Ullman and Bibi Andersen. One of Emir's impressive stories dealt with his unexpected encounter with a Bergman diva: in Paris, taking a seat in a movie theater, he quickly realized that the perfumed arm next to his belonged to the exquisite Ingrid Thulin, who recently had appeared in Visconti's *The Damned*. This subversive, disturbing film focuses on the decline of an affluent German family during the Third Reich, a family that made its fortune on the production of steel and yielded to the pressures of the Nazi regime. Thulin's supporting actors included the androgynous Helmet Berger and Dirk Bogarde, both men exuding a seductive perversity, or vice versa.

Despite our generation gap, Emir and I both shared a sense of being orphans, and we were in a way, both having lost parents when we were young. He had lost his country and, during his years in New Haven, soon to be divorced once again, was distanced—and not only spatially—from family. As a couple, we knew that with our age difference we had a rough road ahead. In our letters, when we were separated for weeks by his travel to Europe or South America, this gap was a leitmotif amid affirmations of love and passion.

It came down to this: upon the advice of my sister Alice and her husband Ben, I was seeing a psychiatrist—there was a special program at Columbia Med School and you could be analyzed practically for nothing—but Emir felt that he was also part of the cure. He convinced me (and himself) that I needed a confident and accomplished man like him to lead the way. In his exiled condition as a displaced person in a new environment, he felt he was renewing his life with a young woman, and I felt, at least for a time, the joy of being a woman and consort to this brilliant man, feeling secure in what felt like my first adult relationship.

Emir's background had its shadows. As a teenager Emir had suffered a nervous breakdown after discovering, in 1940 at the age of nineteen, that he was illegitimate and that the man he thought was his father was a stepfather. His mother asked her brother to tell him the whole story, a painful revelation. The young Emir then physically attacked his uncle because he was told that his real father had been shot in the stomach by this uncle—a crime justified because he was defending the honor of his sister—and left to die alone, an agony that lasted for two days. The helpless rage that Emir must have felt against his father who abandoned his mother, countered by his anger at his uncle for killing the father he would never know, had to be overwhelming.

He revealed this story to me in one of our last conversations in 1985. Why hadn't he told me before? I could only think that such a tragedy must have been a deep source of guilt and shame, not easy to confess to a lover or even to intimate friends. This may be one reason why he started writing his memoirs so late, when he was already seriously ill with colon cancer, and why, sadly, only one volume of the seven planned was completed and published, posthumously.

*

To educated readers in the Hispanic world in the 1960s, Emir Rodríguez Monegal was a well-respected man of letters, and to his enemies, mainly academics, a controversial gadfly in the Latin American politico-literary world. From one day to the next, *Mundo Nuevo* ("New World") had pushed him into the limelight of the Cuban Revolution, divided by writers who supported Fidel Castro and writers who were critical of Stalinist policies of censorship and persecutions which Fidel endorsed and imposed. An anarchist by nature and at heart, as was Borges, Emir defined himself as a liberal socialist.

This political stance meant different things in different camps: he was a radical leftist in Uruguay when right-wing fascist dictatorships took control of Uruguay and Argentina as well as Chile in the 1970s. But he was right-wing or an enemy of the Cuban Revolution because his Paris-based journal *Mundo Nuevo* was being backed by the Ford Foundation and competed with Cuba's *Casa de las Americas* for the same readership.

I earnestly sympathized with Emir's political plight and, through the screen of his narratives of the political landscape then, acquired a jaundiced view of academic life (which I still have) even before I completed my Ph.D. and began my career as a professor. In hindsight, however, it is also now clear that Emir, like many of his generation, was naïve about how to handle politics. He felt the funding behind the journal in no way biased the content of which he and his editors had total control. Naïve idealism was typical of intellectuals then, for example, in the case of his nemesis Angel Rama, who had been his closest boyhood friend, and also like the writer Julio Cortázar whose short stories stand the test of time far more than his political novels—and, let's face it—even like the ill-fated Ernesto "Che" Guevara himself.

Emir's strong suit was his erudite and lucid critical talent. An intuitive, creative reader of texts, he was also inspiring because he firmly defended the freedom of the writer's imagination. Especially at the beginning of our relationship, Emir was a strong supporter of my early academic projects and my trajectory as a translator. From our first conversations I felt that he could see things that others couldn't, like a scanner revealing subtle layers in the art of narrative. As a young man in England, he had studied with F.R. Leavis and his distinguished spouse Queenie, hence began as a "New Critic." Emir was over the years open to diverse theoretical perspectives but mostly had his own original system of reading the labyrinths of the writerly mind; he was someone I could believe in, a true mentor, more brilliant than any man I had been close to until then, and maybe even since then.

Women in the academic and international social circles we inhabited were drawn to him, his dynamic personality and Latin charm. He was by no means an Adonis, but his confident warmth enveloped, even sheltered me, under the spell of his inquisitive yet compassionate dark eyes. There was a bit of George Bernard Shaw's *Pygmalion* in our story, as well as Theodore Dreiser's *Sister Carrie*. Maybe even a hint of Thomas Mann's *The Magic Mountain*, my favorite book read in college, with the feisty yet enigmatic Madame Chauchat. The guileless Hans Castorp falls madly in love partly because her high cheekbones evoke a mysterious Slavic classmate named Hippe with whom he had been obsessed as a boy. Madame Chauchat becomes young Castorp's first mentor in the art of life as well as his adored torment.

Comparing real life with novels and films is a way for me, or any spectator or reader, to step back, to glimpse the truths behind appearances, which is also the overarching premise of Manuel Puig's novels. He would reveal the avatars of Emma Bovary in General Villegas, the rural Argentine town in the pampas where he was born, where women like his mother lived in soap opera fantasies so as not to face the harsh truths of their limited or repressive existence.

During the years we lived together, Emir's literary life directed our travels, mostly to cities—not only to Caracas, Rio de Janeiro and Buenos Aires, Latin American cities with great monuments and great poverty, but to Paris and London several times, where we paid visits to every museum and attended concerts and especially fabulous theater in London, watching, spellbound, Laurence Olivier, Joan Plowright, Rachel Roberts, Albert Finney, John Gielgud, Ralph Richardson and Alec Guinness, just to mention a few of those celebrated British actors. Those times seem so precious now, our visits to enchanting

European cities including Barcelona (now sadly overrun and not as authentic as then) where our days together mingled with the lives of exiled and/or cosmopolitan writers such as Severo Sarduy, Edgardo Cozarinsky, Carlos Fuentes, Mario Vargas Llosa, Guillermo Cabrera Infante, and others, artists as well as writers.

By the time I was returning from Bogotá in September 1968, I had made inroads on my own in the New York literary world of poets, publishers and academics, but as a partner Emir opened doors for me to become a translator. Meeting Manuel Puig in late 1969 led me to editor-in-chief John Macrae III at E.P. Dutton (whom we called Jack) who at the time was publishing Borges in new translations, just as with Guillermo Cabrera Infante I would meet another prestigious publisher at that time, Cass Canfield, Jr., senior editor of Harper & Row which, years later, metamorphosed into the larger and more commercial HarperCollins.

Like the son of another prestigious publisher that I've known who followed in a dominant father's footsteps, I felt that Cass, a polite and amiable guy, tended to be a bit tentative. He had the smarts to publish *One Hundred Years of Solitude* but I think the influence of his assertive Italian (and young) wife Gabriella was important. She had a wise literary guru named Pipina Prieto, an intense Argentine woman from Borges's circle, who at the time was teaching Spanish at Sarah Lawrence College. I learned this intricate story years later when I moved to Santa Barbara and by chance met Pipina, who had renamed herself Allegra after the death of her second husband, Peter Lewis, an electronic composer who also happened to be uncle to actress Juliette Lewis. Pipina died in 2003 and at her wish we cast her ashes into the sea. She was a classic Argentine in that she was relentlessly critical. She and I found that we had much in common, including Adolfo Bioy Casares—she the more fortunate perhaps as she had known, in the beautiful biblical sense, a younger Bioy.

Emir's critical instincts, again, were a beacon that led to my earliest published translations, of two exiled Cuban writers, one straight and one gay, namely, Guillermo Cabrera Infante and Severo Sarduy, and two Argentines, one gay and one straight, Manuel Puig and Adolfo Bioy Casares. Elsewhere I have discussed in depth the masterworks of these exceptional writers, these four, respectively from Havana and Buenos Aires, cities that resonated with the urban energy and cosmopolitan spirit of New York. One of the last times I saw Adolfo Bioy Casares, he confessed to me that my move to the west didn't compute for him. He always pictured me in New York City. Emir had another way of putting it: I was a "pavement flower" and a clear demonstration was our walking visit around the palace of Versailles in the summer of '69. After several days in Paris, I was delighted to see an open field, and eagerly took off romping through the wild flowers and tall grass: oblivious to bucolic realities, I immediately found myself, very uncomfortably, in a swamp of thorns and thistles.

Even before he returned to Europe in November 1968, to see his family and to declare his definitive separation with his wife Magdalena, we started living together in New Haven in his apartment on York Street with its maroon-colored floral design on the bedroom wallpaper. When we moved into that apartment, we decided to keep the kitschy bordello-style wallpaper as a way of winking at the image some people had of us as deviant miscreants. He also shared with me my Waverly Place pad in New York, which weathered both a robbery and a fire during my tenure. The Village then was a bit rundown, not the gentrified overpriced zone it is now.

Around that time, at a party for Octavio Paz at the Center or CIAR (which is now called, with a more neutral tone, the Americas Society), I met another precocious translator, who is today also a distinguished essayist, two years younger than me, Eliot Weinberger. A clever wispy young man, Eliot was a brilliant mixture of Zen master and Woody Allen. We were the only people under forty in that group and our first conversation went something like this:

Eliot (alluding to Emir, artlessly asked):   "Is that your father?"

Me (piqued):   "No, he is my mother."

As he had a mischievous sense of humor, I felt he was a wise guy trying to vex me on purpose, as he was one of those who didn't trust anyone over thirty. Like Bruce Benderson who I met a few years later, Eliot, thanks to a well-heeled family, had the privilege to devote himself entirely to crafting his literary life in the big city or, as Manuel Puig always called it, Gotham.

The writer Donald Barthelme, a cleverly original fiction writer and literary luminary who, like Susan Sontag, taught in the English department at CCNY, lived on 11th Street in a four-story walk-up where several writers lived and formed a sort of commune, shared the following sentiment with me in this regard. One day we were complaining about the time spent teaching instead of writing, and he made the caustic remark that "the smart people are those who inherit money."

As early as 1972 I was contributing translations to CUNY's *Fiction* magazine, sending in my first translations-in-progress of Puig and Sarduy. I became a steady contributor to *Fiction* through my friendship with editor Mark Mirsky and Faith Sales, and continue to contribute to the magazine today. Mark Mirsky, the editor-in-chief of the magazine, had the sense to seek out the latest writing not only by North Americans and Europeans but also the new South American writers; a dear friend (also his talented wife Inger, designer of the journal) he and I remain steadfast readers of the magnificent Uruguayan, Juan Carlos Onetti. At the Fiction parties I got to know Donald, who had the air of an overgrown elf and was very witty, and also Susan Sontag, Jerome Charyn, Fred Tuten and other novelists of the Fiction Collective based in CUNY.

Relationships go through a honeymoon phase, which would be one way to consider what happened after the first six or eight months when I was in love with Emir and exuberantly discovering a new world. The feeling that Emir was like a parent started to weigh upon me and attenuate the passion: why wasn't I on my own or with a companion my own age, like some of my New York peers? I had to reckon with the reality that my literary chums, mostly male such as Eliot and Bruce, still had parents who provided financial support, and, as freewheeling hippies or bohemians, they could afford cavalier attitudes.

On the other hand, despite my gnawing conflicts, I evidently had the sense, too, that I was living a special time with Emir, who was very loveable, and with whom I was immersed, in New York, New Haven or on our travels, in a rarefied Latin American but also European or Europeanized world of writers, scholars and artists, in brief, in an intense environment of high culture and of exciting people, a number of whom became my lifelong friends. As a New Yorker with creative ambitions and as Emir's mate I became a part of this world, at least marginally.

In the summer of 1970 Emir had been invited to a major conference in Caracas, Venezuela. That mega gathering of academics, publishers and poets was an ongoing bacchanalia, endless cocktail parties in that chaotic sprawling Latin American city which seemed to be, with its stretching avenues of speeding cars and polluted air, a third-world version of Los Angeles. The only possible way to get around was by chauffeur-driven vehicle, to those receptions in embassies or mansions in upscale residential enclaves in which academics and literary celebrities mingled, and where the scotch flowed. Even if you weren't finished with your drink, the mobile waiter—surely a bit tipsy himself—in the blink of an eye would extract the old drink from your hand and replace it with a fresh jiggling whiskey on the rocks.

Before our next stop south, the high point of the Venezuelan visit was an invitation to a high-powered midday banquet (the Latin midday was three in the afternoon) in honor of the great Pablo Neruda, at the contemporary and imposing multi-leveled mansion of the novelist Miguel Otero Silva. Miguel Otero Silva was not only wealthy but a member of the Communist party, and also a generous and fair-minded comrade to his literary friends regardless of personal politics. Before the feast officially began, Emir showed me around the grounds, and we admired the large sculpture of a reclining nude woman by Henry Moore in the garden on one of the several moderne levels. In my homey naivete I was almost shocked that such a masterpiece was someone's private property. I mean, I knew of the Medicis and patrons of the arts, but this was the first time I saw a major modern sculpture as a personal possession. It was then that I heard from Emir the term "champagne communist" and its synonym "armchair Marxist" or vice versa.

In the early 1970s Emir was working in Paris on the French version of his biography of Borges with Editions du Seuil, the small, distinguished press run by Severo Sarduy's wealthy French lover François Wahl whose brother was a philosopher, and where Severo worked as Spanish acquisition editor. In Paris, summer of 1970, we had a cheerful reunion with Severo and François. Upon meeting me, the elegant, shy and aloof Frenchman had proclaimed: "Mais, c'est une Renoir!" alluding to those rosy girls in Renoir's lush paintings: how could one not adore being with these individuals? Another gay Cuban in Paris, Ramón Alejandro, then a handsome and successful painter of what could be described as monstrous sex machines, called François "the mummy" because he was so stuffy next to sexy effeminate Severo Sarduy, who had pouting lips and moved his wiry body like a rhumba dancer.

In the summer of 1973 before I returned on my own to France, I went with Emir to Mexico for the first time. This first encounter was a discovery of incredible riches, from the impressive sites of Teotihuacan and Chichén-Itzá to centuries of extraordinary architecture, art and culture and, of course, the vital present of Mexico's City literary life and the arts. After I moved to California, I would continue to develop my own literary and academic world in Mexico in the 1990s and beyond. A famous collector of archeological pieces Emir and I met, whose name I don't remember, gave us a wonderful gift, the ancient sculpture of a female dog who had been buried with her master. Years later, after Emir and I separated, the immortal companion remained with Emir and goodness knows where it ended. I would have liked to have kept this beautiful canine souvenir.

In Mexico we met with both new and legendary artists and writers, among them the great Octavio Paz and poet José Emilio Pacheco, and Gustavo Saínz

Figure 3.3 Severo Sarduy, Jill, François Wahl, and Lydia Rubio at Lydia's apartment, New York City, 1980–81. (Photo credit: Emir Rodríguez Monegal.)

who at that time was an inventive young novelist along the "pop" lines of Cabrera Infante and Manuel Puig and, like them, a major film buff. Gustavo had dark skin, sad eyes and a playful sense of irony. As we sat in the living room of his *tres moderne* Mexico City apartment, we admired Gustavo's impressive film library. He and his young wife at the time, Rosa, were lovely hosts, and Gustavo insisted on taking us on a day excursion to teach me how to ride a motor scooter!

His novels were hip and "pop" portraits of contemporary Mexico, notably his most successful book *Gazapo* and *The Princess of the Iron Palace*. I translated a chapter of the latter for *Fiction* magazine (CUNY) and Gustavo was kind to publish in "Bellas Artes" an attempt of mine at historical fiction in the style of Manuel Puig called "Papa's Funeral"; it was based on research I had begun about the childhood of Evita Peron, who had come from the same region where Manuel Puig had been born. The last time I saw Gustavo was in 2010 at the University of Indiana where he had been teaching after he left Mexico, a long story involving, I believe, cultural politics. Sometime later I learned sadly that he had Parkinson's disease and died in 2015.

But back to June 1973 in Mexico. The amazing sites included the cathedral in downtown Mexico City, built upon the ruins of a pyramid in the great Zocalo square, the "Media Luna" that exquisite café whose dark wood-paneled walls were lined with portraits of Sor Juana. We stopped for another lunch at the famous, blue-tiled Sanborn's cafeteria, and visited the great murals, the palace of

Bellas Artes, the colonial and art deco architecture—it is hard to summarize the grandeur of Mexico City in one paragraph. After dining one night with Octavio Paz and others at "Bellinghausen" a time-honored German restaurant in the Zona Rosa, Octavio and Marie Jo, his dynamic French wife from Corsica, invited us for a nightcap at their apartment on Rio Lerma Street.

Octavio and Marie Jo had met in 1965 in New Delhi, India, while he was then the Mexican ambassador and she was married to another ambassador, and it was love at first sight. Emir's friends in the vibrant vortex of Mexico City were of course Octavio as well as Carlos Fuentes and other writers, poets, artists and filmmakers; at that time Octavio and Carlos were the most world-famous literary figures of Mexico. Our most amusing or, more precisely, surreal visit, was to the home of artist José Luis Cuevas, Luis Buñuel's neighbor in the fashionable district of San Angel Inn.

Cuevas was as crazy (and apparently promiscuous) as he was handsome, and the obsessive conversation topic were his and Buñuel's quarrels about a leaky roof with their shared architect Teodoro, the husband of poet Ulalume Gonzalez de Leon, a petite sharp-featured woman of great intensity. Ulalume, whom we also visited, came from a distinguished Uruguayan family of poets—as her

Figure 3.4 José Luis Cuevas, Emir Rodríguez Monegal, and Jill, Mexico City, 1973. (Photo credit: Cuevas's wife Berta.)

Poe-inspired name suggests—and she was very proud to be the wife of the Mexican architect even if the roofs of the houses he built for Buñuel and Cuevas had leaks. Ulalume was described succinctly by Manuel Puig as being in a "perpetual state of poetic erection." There was such an abundance of poets in the Hispanic world that Manuel couldn't help poking a bit of bitchy fun.

Four years later, when I moved to Cambridge, Massachusetts to begin my first full-time teaching job, Emir and I were no longer domestic partners. But our basic relationship seemed to remain; he was a kindred spirit, almost like a beloved family member. Over the years I got to know his two older children, Georgina and Joaquin, especially Joaquin, a psychotherapist. Joaquin, who resembles his father, helped me come to terms with my feelings of not only loss but guilt, after Emir's death. From his son's perspective, Emir, despite his wonderfulness, was neither the perfect father nor were his relations with women unproblematic. Georgina, a left-wing activist who Emir, with the help of Octavio Paz, saved from torture and political imprisonment in Uruguay, joined the expatriate community of South American revolutionaries in Sweden, married and had children with a Swedish man. Georgina, my age, died of cancer some years ago, but I still have hopes of meeting up with Joaquin again. He (a few years younger) and I fell into a warm friendship when we first met and we have managed to keep the connection alive as of this writing.

Emir and I stayed in close touch during my years in Boston, and at one point, with his friend and literary collaborator, the Brazilian poet and critic Haroldo de Campos, we visited the influential Russian theorist Roman Jakobson at his Cambridge home, by then ancient but still amazingly lucid. Haroldo had a jolly presence; he and Emir animated each other, and conversations were stimulating. We had Easter Sunday dinner with Jakobson and his wife, a Polish linguist, and Jakobson, who was around ninety years old and looked it, downed the many ritual or customary shots of both Polish and Russian vodka without a blink. He and la Pomorska were eager to know which vodka we preferred. I don't remember this discussion as, after the second round of shots, I was quite dizzy and almost fell off my chair.

Haroldo de Campos, who died in 2003, was and still is considered the Brazilian James Joyce. In 1978 together we translated one of his untranslatable Galaxias, based on a crib or literal translation by Jon Tolman, the book consists of fifty prose poems à la *Finnegans Wake*. Haroldo and I did a bilingual recording of it which Haroldo included in his lectures at various universities apparently to the delight of his audiences. It felt creative to work with a Romance language I knew much less but whose meanings I could nonetheless fathom, and to work with the poet who applauded my sound-is-sense approach. Creative projects like this alleviated my first year as an assistant professor was 1977-78, the year Emir and Haroldo visited; I was terrified by the whole package of teaching challenges upon undertaking my first tenure-track job at Tufts University. Especially at the beginning, it was an overwhelming task, but Emir reassured me, reminding me that I had already given lectures and taught translation workshops, and that I would become a very good teacher.

After Emir's death in November 1985, Manuel Puig reminisced how proud Emir had been of me. During our years together, however, Emir would also caution me on occasion that I didn't have the patience of a scholar, that I was good at whatever I set my mind to do, but "you're a bit scattered, my dear," he'd say, meaning I was too dispersed to devote endless hours to the minutia of research. In hindsight we often see that rigorous criticism can be more helpful than boundless praise, can stimulate us to go the extra mile. At the time, Emir's criticism made a big impact on me: for years I made great sacrifices in the arena of personal relationships to overcome my defects as it were. One could say that work became my religion.

I wondered, later, if noting my "dispersed" tendency, while true in some ways, wasn't also a projection of his own self-criticism. After all, among his academic rivalries, he had been disparaged maliciously as facile, as a mere "journalist" by a former boyhood friend, the venerated Uruguayan scholar Angel Rama, who (as mentioned earlier) became Emir's archenemy. Rama was a Marxist/ sociological literary critic, while Emir's signature or at least early approach was New Criticism which promoted art's autonomy and individuality—the text has rules, that is, a life its own. Emir's critical approaches evolved and changed as new theories emerged with their specific lingo, which impressed me at the same time I agreed with his sense that scholars often were (and surely still are) insufferable academics who felt that unless your writing style is desiccated, unreadable and weighted down with jargon, it's not "serious."

Didn't he, Emir, deep down where he didn't go, want to be a fiction writer? He said no, that more than anything, he was a voracious reader, that was what he loved more than anything. A literary critic is not necessarily a scholar in a strict sense, just as a scholar does not necessarily qualify as a critic. Emir bridged both worlds, as did the famous critic and writer Edmund Wilson whose essays in the 1960s influenced the Anglo-American literary world and of course English departments. "Bunny" Wilson was a creative writer as well as a critic, and Emir's various biographies of great writers, and especially the first (and only completed) volume of his memoirs that came out after his death, prove that he was not only an important critic but also had the voice of a gifted storyteller.

In any case, the Cold War drew a line in the sand that was impossible to ignore, and, if you were at all critical of Castro, you were right-wing. No dialogue would be possible, an insidious censorship which today still prevails although the terms have changed, degrading the level of public discourse to absurd depths. Emir died at a time when the Cold War—which some of us thought was ending, along with the political evils of mendacious smear campaigns—was merely changing form, morphing not only in academe but in global geopolitics. The Berlin Wall came down in 1989 and fascism/totalitarianism found another ally in late capitalism; the digital wall of media indoctrination rose to sustain this injurious alliance. The computer is a miraculous invention that helps our lives but, like all technological progress, takes its toll.

Emir died of cancer in November 1985, a distressing rapid decline and death after the first unfortunate symptoms in February of that year. I had recently moved across the country to the University of Washington in Seattle—and had just organized early that February an invitation to bring Emir out to give a lecture. The phone call that he was too ill to travel because they had discovered that he had an advanced stage of colon cancer was a shock that threw me into a panic. It was devastating to all who admired or loved him, students and colleagues at Yale, friends everywhere in the U.S., Europe and, of course, South America. Ghostly feelings of the devastation of my mother's death resurfaced with the anguish of loss, or overwhelming feelings of fear, abandonment and even anger at the injustice of it all, which were reawakened when Emir was dying. Such feelings have diminished with time, but I think they will always remain with me.

Our separation as domestic partners, in 1976, before my move to Cambridge and Tufts University, had been very upsetting, so much so that it happened in stages over three or four years, with much grief along the way. In our last telephone conversation, I tried in vain to hide my sadness and said to him things like, "You can't go, you are the center of my life" to which he replied with a weakened but still warm voice, "You are your center," trying to bolster me when he was the one who was dying.

Deathly ill, Emir made a final trip back to Uruguay with his partner Selma, a lovely Brazilian woman he married in that last month to provide for her as well as his children. This must have been a superhuman effort on his part as he was so frail and emaciated by then, but the loving and enthusiastic reception he received in Montevideo was extremely important to him, a final reconciliation, after two decades of exile, with his country, with what family remained, and of course with a few dear old friends.

I regret that I couldn't join them on that final journey, to see Emir's long-awaited reunion with his compatriots, and to see again some of his friends I knew and for whom I felt a fond affection. Alas, Emir didn't get to see how I came into my own. Realizing projects inspired by his early influence, I like to think that he would have been proud of my biography of Manuel Puig or the five-volume Penguin classics series of Borges's poetry and non-fictions for which I served as General Editor. Emir was an invaluable guiding presence for me in my twenties, and in a way, he is always present. I did miss out on a more normal or "youthful" early adulthood. I have had regrets about this, but what I gained was precious to my growth in many ways, certainly as a translator, a critic and professional academic. Emir was one of a kind, without any doubt, and I hold as precious too those remaining friends who share with me his memory.

4

Swinging London with Cabrera Infante

It was mid-February 1969 when I flew to London to meet Emir and we celebrated St. Valentines day in the Vanderbilt Hotel. A few days later we took a train (trains in the UK still had a quaint charm then) for a weekend in seaside Brighton, home of the Regency Palace; Brighton was a regal resort during the eighteenth and nineteenth centuries and still had swanky neighborhoods, but post-war Brighton felt more like Coney Island as a cheap beach vacation for the working class, immortalized in the 1950s in Lawrence Olivier's film *The Entertainer*.

Because it was the dead of winter, Emir had no trouble finding us elegant lodgings, in the Grand Hotel along the promenade facing the Channel, but our very noticeable age difference embarrassed me if no one else, so that I tried futilely to make myself invisible by wearing my winter cap over my eyes and stuffing my hands deep into my coat pockets. I couldn't help feeling, as suggested earlier, that we looked like Lolita and Humbert Humbert when we registered at the front desk where we discovered that, aside from a congregation of oceanographers from China, we were the only guests. Our guest quarters were a warm ample Victorian refuge from the freezing cold outside, and I remember reclining in a huge bathtub, smoking pot and inviting Emir to try the forbidden herb—I believe that was the only time he ever tried it, mainly to humor me.

We were both glad to get back to bustling London, which had a special place in Emir's heart, the first European city he got to know in the early 1950s, still partly in ruins from the Second World War. In this post-war London he had a passionate affair with a married Englishwoman, an artist, who did a beautiful portrait of him; her name was Dodie, and their love affair was, I believe, a key to Emir's Anglophilia. On a research fellowship at the British Museum in 1951, the young Emir had gone to investigate the topic of his first and longest scholarly book. The subject was Andres Bello (1781–1865), a leading Latin American intellectual, philosopher and educator in the nineteenth century. London was delightful during our early visits. As Emir knew and loved the city well—he returned often, especially when living in Paris from 1965–68—he was the perfect guide that February of 1969. I must mention a Gracie Allen or, if you wish, a Jean Harlow moment when, on the first day Emir and I strolled around the neighborhood of Kensington, I exclaimed with enthusiasm, "Why, this reminds me of the colonial architecture in New England!" We immediately looked at each other and burst out laughing at my lapse.

Emir's English friends were amusing with the eccentricities they were famous for, especially a charmingly outspoken Anglo-Uruguayan lady named Elsie Crombie, married to a distinguished curator of colonial art, a classic-looking white-haired Brit. Elsie and her art-collecting husband had a tastefully luxurious London residence, and she was an irrepressible storyteller. I remember her very particular reaction to Neruda when she got to know him, describing the portly poet as "such a pet!"

She also was responsible for spreading an alarming story Emir hastened to correct. She had heard from the well-respected historian George Pendle, author of Penguin's paperback classic volume on Latin American history, who had misheard from a mutual Uruguayan friend that Emir was in "jail." We went to have lunch with Pendle, yet another distinguished-looking white-haired Brit, at the famous Savoy where Oscar Wilde used to be a regular patron—a thrilling detail—and Emir hastened to clarify to the bemused Pendle, that unlike the tragic figure of Wilde he had not been in jail. Their mutual friend had pronounced "Yale" with his regional accent, changing the "Y" to a soft "J."

Shortly after I arrived in London, Emir took me to meet the famous new Cuban or rather "Havanan" writer Guillermo Cabrera Infante and his wife Miriam Gomez in their cozy flat at 53 Gloucester Road, a street with columned row houses in what was then the posh borough of Kensington. As a total urbanite, Guillermo preferred not to be labeled as a Cuban writer not only because he was a political exile, dismissed from his post as Cuba's cultural attaché in Brussels, but because he strongly felt his identity was as a native of Havana. He had first fled to Spain in 1965, where he was branded a communist even though he had been cast out of Cuba as a traitor to the communist cause. He sought and found asylum, or at least a home to call his own, in England. His fall from grace was a curious paradox which taught me and others about the farce of politics, and I could see why he and Emir were close friends and very supportive of each other during those turbulent years.

In the 1960s the city was now swinging London, particularly Soho and Chelsea, and had decidedly been given a new look, but the city still retained its prewar charms. A few blocks from their flat you could stroll around the lovely

Kensington Gardens with the Peter Pan statue, which took you to the well-known green of Hyde Park, adorned with the bronze statues of characters from *Alice in Wonderland*. This famous children's book was a fount of inspiration to Guillermo's most groundbreaking novel *Tres tristes tigres*, which was the first book I translated, in "closelaboration" with the author—this neologism was the happy invention of Cabrera Infante who wanted to sign our collaborative translation as a "closelaboration," but the publisher claimed sole power over the title page, hence no neologism. This book, which captured Havana better than any book since (or before), translated into polyglot Spanish the brilliant political satires of Lewis Carroll. Like *Alice in Wonderland* and *Through the Looking Glass*, *TTT*, as Guillermo liked to call it, gives the reader the sense of a world gone mad, an upside-down world where the only sense was non-sense.

We rang the bell and Guillermo's actress wife Miriam opened the door, greeted us effusively and escorted us down a narrow hallway bedecked with photographs and books. Tall, dark-haired in a slinky long dress, Miriam was very Cuban, that is, very assertive, as well as glamorous with a slight resemblance to Ava Gardner. Miriam led us to Guillermo's den that faced onto a shady back garden. Among the fascinating photos along the walls of the flat was a black-and-white blow-up of Guillermo and Miriam in the living room, taken by his friend the celebrated Cuban photographer Jesse Fernandez. In a natty three-piece suit, veddy British, but at the same time short and squat, Guillermo is seated with one leg crossed over the other, the usual Havana cigar between his lips, and Miriam stands proudly behind him, the two of them looking like a chic celebrity couple in swinging London mode.

The den itself was fittingly decorated with striped tiger wallpaper in homage to those night owls who prowl around Havana for five hundred pages, those sad, funny and unforgettable paper tigers in Guillermo's most famous book. Sitting on a divan was Guillermo, impeccably attired, his general appearance a cross between a squat toad and a Buddhist god, his brown Cuban countenance at once delicate and comical, charismatic and poker-faced, his mustache à la Pancho Villa, but so very hip and urbane. The two friends, Emir and Guillermo, had not seen each other for a while, and Miriam was not only amused to see Emir with such a young girlfriend, but also, as she was wearing a long dress, made sure to clarify: "Emir, I am not hiding my legs, they are as beautiful as ever," and she promptly lifted her skirt so that we would see her shapely ankles. Miriam often came out with mostly unintentional, oddly hilarious non-sequiturs: such was her charm. Miriam was also a marvelous cook and made Cuban feasts, not to mention the *cafecito*, the espresso which was a drug Guillermo required at regular intervals.

Guillermo and I shared a propensity for Marx—Groucho and his brothers. Their surreal, absurd, hilarious movies like *Duck Soup* and *A Night at the Opera* were a strong defense against the banalities of reality. Almost immediately upon this first meeting, Guillermo and I seemed to collide harmoniously in wordplay, as if we were personifying Groucho and company. He was struggling with the translation of *TTT*, and during that visit he would happily decide that I was the native English-speaking soulmate/co-translator *TTT* needed.

Guillermo was brilliantly funny but also very wise. He was as Cuban as Desi Arnaz, despite himself, and from the very beginning, whenever I or any young female were around, he engaged in a kind of non-stop and mostly non-referential flirtation, but thankfully Guillermo preferred blondes, so we had a purely platonic and mostly affectionate friendship. His 1950s Hollywood dream girl was Angie Dickinson, especially in the stylish gangster movie *Point Blank* as Lee Marvin's mistress. In any case Miriam kept him on a tight leash, tied to his writing and her cooking. Our conversation that wintry afternoon in London, so distant in every way from the island of their Havana, led us to the topic of the translation he was trying to complete with his collaborator, an English poet named Donald Gardner.

The elite editor Cass Canfield, Jr., of Harper & Row in New York was anxiously awaiting the manuscript. Guillermo wanted the English version to retain the wit and humor of the spoken words in the original Spanish or, more aptly, in the "Cuban." Guillermo spread out for me, on the dining room table, a few pages of the translation draft from sections of the book titled "The Debutants" and "She Sang Boleros." It was quickly apparent that the language had to be more "cut to the chase" colloquial, more vulgar American, to duplicate the effect of rapid shorthand banter and the many double entendres in Guillermo's perfect impersonations of the voices of Havana in this autobiographical novel.

The three or five main characters were avatars of himself in love with Miriam, now insulated in their Cuban island flat Gloucester Road. Overwriting the street slang of Havana with New York-sounding quips and fast rhythms was a fruitful strategy for the translation. With Guillermo's encouragement, during that first visit I went over a few pages to "slangify" or to shape more speedy and colorful sentences. Pleased at my revisions, he made a long-distance call to Cass Canfield in New York and our collaboration began.

Months later, I was invited to lunch in a fashionable midtown restaurant by Cass when Guillermo could join us in New York. Cass, of course, looked upon the young me with suspicion: was I a chick Guillermo was after? Despite these initial doubts regarding Guillermo's motives, Cass soon realized that I was a translator, not his paramour. We would collaborate mostly by mail, and the correspondence (now in a vault at the Lilly Library in Bloomington, Indiana) is filled with the unbridled wordplay that overflowed from *Tres tristes tigres* into *Three Trapped Tigers*.

This satirical masterpiece was well-receive but was also disparaged ungenerously in *The New Yorker* by John Updike who revealed his double standard. Rather than a Cuban version of Joyce's *Ulysses*, he had been hoping for a traditional or even social realism. It was as if a Cuban novelist should limit him or herself to being a historian or anthropologist, as if the only reason to read a book from Cuba, from Updike's point of view, was to learn about the culture of the island country. What he didn't seem to realize was that nothing could be more Cuban and certainly more Havanan than *TTT*. Updike should have noted that Groucho was the Marxist closest to Guillermo Cabrera Infante's heart as the writer was a Cuban son of Marxists infuriated with Castro because of his Stalinist-style censorship. Guillermo shared Groucho's deep skepticism. For Groucho as for other brilliant comedians, the world seemed filled with fools and scoundrels, and life a minefield of letdowns, so why not turn angst into hilarity? The most authentic way for Cabrera Infante to deal with his and Cuba's tragic history and polemicized present in the 1960s was Groucho Marx's farcical approach in which sense and non-sense were on an equal plane.

This is where I came in (as they used to say in movie theaters with continuous showings), thanks in part to my familiarity with, and delight in, Groucho's irrepressible verbal anarchism in which nonsense made more sense. It was also very possible that Groucho, in turn, had been motivated not only by his family experience in vaudeville but also by the Reverend Dodgson, better known as Lewis Carroll. Guillermo wrote about our translation in *Review* magazine in 1971 in an article where he concludes that I had "that Jewish New York sense of humor that expresses itself in wordplay and faces reality with a strict verbal logic."

Emir, a Cartesian thinker as he had been educated in a French school in Uruguay, was our devoted fan but also sometimes lost his patience when we gathered, and puns invasively punctuated the conversation. Guillermo needed comedy to make light of weighty and, for him, tragic circumstances: language play was an escape from the noirish nadir of exile, and his polyglot jokes were bilingual subversions. In that moment, I already knew that beneath Cabrera Infante's compulsive punning ran a deeper undercurrent. In his opposition to

Castro's repressive measures, he felt like a loner, like Gary Cooper in *High Noon*, one of his (and Emir's) favorite movies whose screenwriter Carl Foreman had been blacklisted during the McCarthy era.

This film had a not-so-hidden message regarding Cold War politics in the United States in the 1950s: Cooper's character, a retired sheriff defending justice, was misunderstood by friends who became his enemies and who even ganged up on him. A political western, *High Noon* was innovative in its moment. The reversals as well as parallels between film and reality are striking. The Oscar-winning script of *High Noon* was an allegorical western condemning the McCarthy witch-hunts during that infamous decade, but an unfortunate irony is that Hollywood star Gary Cooper was one of those who named names, who betrayed his colleagues in the industry.

That mild winter afternoon when Emir and I first visited the Cabrera Infantes in their Kensington London flat, the discussion and exchange of news focused on politics and the Castro regime's boycott against Latin American intellectuals who disagreed with some of Castro's policies. Cabrera Infante and many close peers had been exiled because they didn't agree with the cultural policies of "el Caballo": Fidel was nicknamed "the Horse." The latest gossip about betrayals among Cubans was a particularly bitter topic of conversation that afternoon.

But, if exile were an ailment, a source of pain, cinema was the antidote and anecdote. Guillermo had a photographic memory for practically every film he had ever seen, and it was our mutual fascination with movies that laid the groundwork for the bond we forged in that den of trapped tigers. Fortunately, humor was a salvation from the grim realities, and Guillermo's spot-on impersonations, as of the elliptical exchange between the tall, lean and elderly Cooper, and the darkly tempestuous Katy Jurado (in those days one of the few Latina stars in Hollywood) in the legendary *High Noon* left us in stitches.

In the scene Guillermo imitated, Gary and Katy, playing characters whose love affair precedes the action of the film, meet in her hotel room for the first and last time in the film. The tall, craggy Cooper, with those light eyes and a will of steel, has sought her out to warn her about the bad guy just released from jail, who was heading their way for swift revenge with his nasty gang. In the hotel, the worried hero also sees in passing his pretty new wife, played by a Grace Kelly so young in the film that, next to Cooper, she looks like a daughter not a bride, waiting for the train because of her Quaker opposition to violence. Even she will be, for a moment, another unwilling traitor ready to abandon her beloved, at first leaving him alone to face his enemies.

In the tense dialogue between Gary and Katy, Guillermo imitates Katy, with her big dark sultry eyes, saying what sounds like "Tanto tiempo sin verde." It was as if an Anglo ear had heard the wrong consonant that changes "verte" to "verde." And so, instead of "It's been so long since I've seen you," the sentence sounds more like, "Such a long time without green." And even worse, when, with noble macho control over his feelings, Gary, equally smoldering, replies with Hemingwayan concision, "See, lo say" instead of "Sí, lo sé." The gringo pronunciation turns the scene's gravitas, unintentionally, into its own parody.

Another of Guillermo's exacting imitations played off another great western, *The Treasure of the Sierra Madre*, in which a captured bandido (who had murdered the vividly paranoid character played so angrily by Humphrey Bogart), hatless as he faces the firing squad, cries out his last wish in Spanish, "Puedo recoger mi sombrero, teniente?" (Can I pick up my hat, Lieutenant?). The lieutenant responds by proceeding to order his soldiers to fire, executing the bad bandit. This film, populated with sly Mexican bandidos and desperate gringo gold-diggers, directed by the legendary John Huston and starring Bogart and the director's famous actor father Walter Huston, was yet another classic. Westerns were where Emir and I parted ways ultimately. Their overblown machismo is doubtlessly the main reason why, even as a child, I found many of them tedious, but we still should credit both the films mentioned here as fine exemplars of the genre.

Guillermo Cabrera Infante, like his newfound friend Manuel Puig, brought his childhood enthusiasm and lifetime devotion to Hollywood movies into his writing. Cabrera Infante was a film critic and journalist before he became a storywriter, and Manuel aspired to write screenplays since his adolescence. They became friends before I met either of them. Their first meeting happened after Guillermo read *La traición de Rita Hayworth*, Manuel's first novel and, like the young novelist and Gallimard acquisitions editor Juan Goytisolo, loved it—especially the clever daring of Rita Hayworth in the title! For Cabrera Infante, the movies were *the* twentieth century art; for Manuel Puig, the film spectator was the ultimate protagonist of his novels. Novels had to do something different now because movies were far superior as storytelling machine, a solitary place of magic that carried spectators on safe adventures away from home but also fed us nostalgia for those places in the past to which we cannot return.

These two writers were nurtured on the movies as kids, the movie house really a haven or temporary paradise for children who were poor or isolated in an oppressive small town. Puig spoke of his early failed career as a film-maker in

Rome as the place he discovered writing and to return to the "paradise" of his childhood excursions to the movies. Though never acknowledged, the cult Italian film *Cinema Paradiso* was inspired by Manuel Puig's first novel, *La traición de Rita Hayworth*. Cabrera Infante's principal books also feed off nostalgia for those afternoon childhood idylls in the darkened theater where life danced on a screen, a time and place traveler, translating us momentarily into a desired past, or a longed-for present or even future.

Thanks to Emir, Guillermo Cabrera Infante and I came to translate together *Tres tristes tigres*, his first novel (1965) and, most will agree, his most important book. He never used the term "novel," which he felt limited the definition of a book that for him transcended the traditional borders of fiction. Along the lines of Freud on jokes and the unconscious, Cabrera Infante's dictum, again was that "puns hide pain." This first collaboration between us was great fun with puns, as the book and our correspondence clearly reveal.

The relationships authors establish with their translators are often different from the way he or she may interact with supportive scholars, perhaps feeling more at ease and therefore willing to open to a translator in ways they would be reluctant to do so with a literary critic. Translation is the closest and, I think, the most intimate reading possible—and it is a collaboration whether the original author is literally present. Our translation followed the original's irreverence by turning proper names inside out and subverting titles. The official censors in a Spain still controlled by Franco's Catholic agenda helped clarify, ironically, what Infante both wanted and didn't want to tell. In English, obscenities parading as allusions in the Spanish version, could proliferate more freely and become more explicit.

While doing a translation a few years ago, I was told by Mexican author Mauricio Figueiras Montiel that some of my queries about the original helped him discover what he originally wanted to write in the original Spanish. This had happened earlier with Cabrera Infante who felt his writing needed to become more expansive in English, thus making fun with, as well as of, English. English led him to engage with his exiled condition in literary terms as well as with his youth in bilingual Havana in an island country overshadowed by the giant to the North.

As Dante did with the Tuscan dialect in the Divine Comedy, *Tres tristes tigres* turned spoken Cuban into a written literary language. A vast canvas of fragments, *TTT*, with all its apolitical playfulness, with all its characters' efforts not to talk about the Cuban Revolution, was described by Guillermo as a "gallery of voices," an explosion of slang and Joycean dislocutions. All that remained of his life in that country was in this book written in a racially mixed Spanish marked by certain streets in Havana, by a specific region and a city with its hidden codes, elaborated polyphonically with hybrid cultural and literary references.

Guillermo Cabrera Infante's penchant for malice aforethought features prominently in one of the visits Emir and I made to Gloucester Road. Guillermo knew that Emir (like many travelers) would be nervous before heading to the airport, and always wanted to get there well ahead of time. But Emir, like Guillermo, also had strong critical opinions, and on this occasion, as Emir and I were heading down the steps to the sidewalk with our luggage, Guillermo persisted in continuing a debate with Emir on who was the greatest American playwright, the southerner Tennessee Williams or New England's Eugene O'Neill. For Guillermo, Williams was more original as the lyrical creator of a compelling worldview with his intense dialogues and monologues and the poignant characters that are so much him and yet universal in their longings and flaws.

Emir, a worthy adversary in any debate, stressed O'Neill's dramatic dialogues and evocative portraits of the members of a tragic New England family, imparting a language that conjured a strong sense of place, a true American idiom, and the eternal battle of men and women. The terms of their arguments curiously were almost identical, so it all came down, really, to a difference in sensibility. Seen from today, I believe that Williams has withstood the passage of time more successfully than O'Neill whose plays have the feel of a period piece. Even though I had enjoyed a brilliant production of "Long Day's Journey into Night" with Colleen Dewhurst and Jason Robards, I still preferred Williams's plays— and maybe even more the film versions, notably Vivien Leigh's painfully vivid performance in *Streetcar Named Desire*. But at the time I wasn't sure, and felt protectively that I didn't want to line up against Emir.

Aside from seeing the work of both writers on stage, for me the Tennessee Williams plays I had seen translated into films were a guilty pleasure, especially with formidably intense and exquisitely beautiful leading ladies like Leigh and Elizabeth Taylor, to whom I, a typical spectator, was attracted. I didn't recognize this as bisexuality or even androgyny, even though I had been considered a bit of a tomboy as a kid, a fast runner with my hair flying in the wind. Vivien Leigh as doomed Blanche Dubois still today is a reminder of my sister Carol, so pretty with her gentile turned-up nose, so hopelessly fragile, neurotic, lost to herself and to others.

The funny side of the Williams vs O'Neill incident was typical of Guillermo's argumentative nature and perverse tendency to make fun usually of someone, in this case at Emir's expense, which seemed ungenerous even though it was amusing. I didn't like playing the role of listener rather than participant in this conversation, but this was often the case during my years with Emir, and was part of what thrust me outward, away from our relationship, to seek out kindred spirits in my own generation. At any rate, the playwright debate raged on as Emir tripped more than once over his suitcase on the sidewalk, determined to reach the impatiently waiting cab. Guillermo got in the last word, exclaiming that the debate was not settled simply because Emir was flying off to another continent.

Around that time, I made the foolish error of connecting my actress sister Carol with Guillermo when, in late 1969, he went to Hollywood for the filming of his screenplay *Vanishing Point*. Carol, already very fragile emotionally when I had last visited her in 1967, did not appreciate his lechery or sexual double entendres, and he thought she was "too touchy." She made him promise that if he ever ran into Ava Gardner, he should ask her who her plastic surgeon was. And so, despite Carol's touchiness and perhaps gallantly, he swore that he would. Sure enough, at a party in an upper-crust London townhouse of one of Guillermo's hip film-maker friends, he told me that he made the mistake of asking Ava Gardner this most insensitive question, to which she responded, "You Sonofabitch!" Apparently, she spent the remainder of the party sitting outside the house on the steps, waving her cocktail glass with drunken fury and cursing at the startled partygoers trying to climb the stairs to get past her into the house.

While a tad annoyed at me or my sister, or both of us, Guillermo was, I think, mainly tickled by the explosive effect of his inopportune query. Moments of levity were frequent around Guillermo, a bookish, razor-sharp contrarian and at times quite cantankerous. One misses those private gatherings, whether in New York, Connecticut, or London, with him and brilliant witty friends like Nestor Almendros, Severo Sarduy, Heberto Padilla and others sadly gone with the wind.

The death of Guillermo's mother's (she and his father were founders of the Cuban Communist Party) in 1972, combined with the enormous pressure from what Mario Vargas Llosa so aptly identifies as "sanitization of his person and of his work" by the pro-Castro government, plunged Guillermo into manic depression and brought about the near loss of his mental balance.[3] Maybe this emotional breakdown was contagious because that year I too (for my own reasons) was going through a bad patch. He was administered over twenty electro-shocks and put on lithium indefinitely. These were, in any case, dark and worrisome times for Guillermo's friends and above all for his wife Miriam.

It was largely thanks to her care and resilience that he was able to recover and continue to write another thirty years until his death. Upon regaining his stability, he wrote a subtle and very original book composed of actual quotations from history books, patriotic song lyrics, often lyrical fragments that were like prose poems, entitled *Vista del amanecer en el trópico* or *View of Dawn in the Tropics*. It is a powerful account made up of fragments and representing Cuba's history as the history of violence, a book at once brutal and refined, tragic and satirical, that begins with the arrival of the Spaniards in the late fifteenth century and portrays elliptically the island's numerous tyrannies from Columbus's time until 1974, the year of the book's publication. This thankfully brief book, challenging of course, was enticing as a translation project—and I was glad to collaborate again with Guillermo, in this case on a text, unlike *Three Trapped Tigers*, that was terse and somber, but also masterfully structured and built upon historical facts, literary allusions and the languages of Cuba from its "discovery" to the era of Fidel.

*

Our final duet, the eight hundred page *La Habana para un Infante difunto*—literally "Havana for a Dead Prince/Infant"—was, to the consternation of his editor Cass Canfield, Jr., a book even bulkier than *TTT*. *La Habana*, its title a wordplay on Ravel's melancholy "Pavane for a Dead Princess," is an auto-fiction, a Proustian memoir of Cabrera Infante's youth in Havana in which the protagonist discovers both sex and his writerly vocation. This humongous book took four years to translate and is titled *Infante's Inferno*.

It was now 1979, an early point in my career as university professor living in Cambridge, Massachusetts, also a very challenging period with my attention divided between teaching and pursuing a translation and literary career. A year earlier I had become involved romantically for the first time with a woman. Her name was Lydia Rubio, and she was Cuban. At the time we met she was an architect working in Cambridge, but was soon to dedicate the rest of her life to the art of painting. We met the first year I was a junior assistant professor living in Cambridge, Massachusetts and teaching at Tufts University. She was teaching at Harvard, and we met by pure chance through mutual acquaintances at the Harvard Faculty Club.

With Lydia I discovered the sensuality of same-sex love, a revelation that partially explained to me my ambivalence about men. Lydia and I have

Figure 4.1 Jill and Lydia Rubio with Nestor Almendros, Boston 1981. (Photo credit: Nestor Almendros.)

maintained, despite ups and downs, an affectionate lifetime friendship. I already had some sense, mostly in an unconscious corner of my brain, that I was attracted to my gender, at Vassar or even earlier. I had crushes but seemed or pretended to be oblivious to this fact. My friendship pattern was always to have one special pal, even in junior high school. These one-on-one friendships were based on significant affinities and shared interests, and mostly a goofy sense of humor, almost a secret world of jokes.

A curious incident in Spain when I was nineteen, with my midwestern roommate Judy, should have alerted me. We were on a class tour to Valencia on the east coast of Spain, for the celebration of Las Fallas Valencianas, a rather scary fiesta which involved big fires burning huge wooden effigies or installations in small squares everywhere. Judy and I had to share a bed in a modest hotel, as most of us students did, though I suppose there were wealthy students who had their own rooms. As we lay there in the dark, I was startled but pretended not to notice that Judy was softly touching my ear. At the time I thought maybe this was some childish habit as if I were a substitute for her blanket, and neither of us said anything about it in the morning.

When I did come close to an affair with a woman while still living in New York City, my feelings of desire were short-circuited by doubts and, in any case,

I was about to leave the city. However, by the time I met Lydia in late January 1978, I had survived almost five lonely months in Cambridge. After the quick, spontaneous pace of life in New York, the Boston atmosphere felt muted, almost puritanical. What I would realize in time is that the move to Massachusetts, stressful as moves often are, prepared me for adapting to other displacements, even further away from New York City, finally "translating" myself, despite reluctance, into a citizen of the West Coast.

*

I have digressed, however, from my final chapter with Cabrera Infante, perhaps because my first lesbian experience coincided with my last translation of Cabrera Infante, and my bisexuality was both accepted and not accepted by Guillermo, whose vision of Havana as a sexual vortex and a liberated world betrayed by Stalinism, was still biased by a deeply grounded machismo.

Add to this his dilemma as an exiled writer. Having lived over fifteen years in England, Guillermo, about to become a full-fledged citizen of the United Kingdom, wanted to earn his own reputation as a writer in English. *Infante's Inferno* more than anything is about his discovery of sex, but from his point of view as a writer this book also showcased his compulsive constructions erected, as he put it, upon the destruction of a sentence, a word, a phoneme, arriving at a transcreation in which proper names, as in the Spanish, were the subjects of linguistic experiments.

In hindsight, it might have been better for me to pass on this bulky 800-page *mamotreto*, because it did lead to our separation as "closclaborators." *Mamotreto*, this perfect word for unwieldy books or massive manuscripts feels untranslatable, but "doorstop" is close. Guillermo's *Inferno* turned to be a battleground in which text and sex intermingled in that (I believe) Guillermo did not favor my experiments which were not related to literary translation. He and I engaged in an intermittent tug of war that lasted four years, with delays on his end mainly, an ongoing battle in which I was trying to extract prose that reflected his witty style despite his baroque experiments with English, with him compulsively generating prolonged wordplays that turned into endless sentences. One obsessive chapter that had taken me months to translate had to be completely removed from the translation to make room for the final chapter which, thanks to his intervention, had virtually doubled in length. Infuriated, I could do nothing but fume about my wasted effort while he smoked his intractable cigar. A veritable "infant's inferno" you will agree, but the book still had its

Proustian merits. Unlike *TTT*, however, its reception in English was relatively lukewarm.

Intelligence and verbal fireworks pervaded all his writing but, in the final reckoning, none of his books would rival the inventive polyvalence, the raw authenticity, the keen wit and profoundly tragic edge of *TTT*. We are immersed richly in the material city of Infante's Infernal Havana in "La Habana for a Dead Prince," but we feel the heady mixture of pre-Revolution angst and the lustful spirit of Havana much more intensely in *TTT*, his first major work. As the *New York Times* reviewer stated in 1971, "I doubt a funnier book has been written in Spanish since Don Quixote."

*

In the final decade of his life, the last time I visited them, the three of us—Guillermo, Miriam and I—took a walk, that is, Miriam asked Guillermo, to "treat me to a literary tour" around Kensington, their lovely neighborhood, so that Guillermo, who had significant health issues, at least (she whispered to me) would get a little exercise. Guillermo was pleased to point out "Henry James lived here," and other celebrity dwellings. This was probably September 2000, when I came to London to promote, with our mutual publisher Faber & Faber, my newly published Puig biography. Before leaving the UK, I took a train from London to Edinburgh where I met up with friends from Santa Barbara and we drove from the literary and gastronomic mecca of Edinburgh to tour the castles, "Lochs" as far as the Isle of Skye, and onward to Glasgow where we took a flight back to London. Scotland's ruined castles and desolate landscapes were magical, as were the civilized evening aperitifs, sipping single malt scotch in provincial inns. I am grateful that the book enabled that little trip with friends.

In his review of the biography, Guillermo gave me generous praise by saying that it brought Manuel Puig, who had died July 1990, back to life—which is the most to which any biographer can aspire. I remember that on that walk in Kensington, Guillermo was no longer the same man. He shuffled rather slowly and seemed thin and fragile, but he was dressed as elegantly as ever, and his beautiful walking cane seemed to cement his place of honor in a neighborhood of literary greats such as Henry James who was a fellow expat as well.

The "flat" at 53 Gloucester Road was no longer the same either, as its swinging London aura had long since faded. I speak of the era when Offenbach, inscrutable Siamese cat, reigned over the house with his loud howls, great cunning and aloof poise. Normally standoffish, Offenbach had an inexplicable crush on Emir and had to be restrained from leaping onto his lap—with his feline instinct he also stubbornly zeroed in on anyone (in this case, me) who had a severe allergy to cat dander.

The very last time I visited 53 Gloucester Road was in 2010, there was only Miriam and another cat, as Offenbach had died in 1978. Guillermo had accumulated so many more books and papers that the once impressive floor to very high ceiling library was spilling over and invading Miriam's kitchen. Guillermo had died of septicemia in a London Hospital in 2005. Our last conversation had been a phone call; I was at home in Santa Barbara, where fifteen years earlier he had given a brilliant talk that was pure performance art titled "To Kill a Foreign Name." A pity we didn't record his lecture, as witty as any delivered by Oscar Wilde on his famous tour of the West. The delivery was impeccable, and Guillermo Cabrera Infante truly could have been a great character actor. Indeed, he had been approached for such by a major Hollywood director, but he said no firmly.

The sad news of Guillermo's death in 2005 reached me by chance, in a newspaper when I was traveling in Argentina with Lydia. The loss of Guillermo was almost like losing a conscientious father who had given me advice and support, and who also, at times, reproached me, sometimes with good reason. When he complained I had too much ego to be a translator, however, this was less for my good than about his alpha maleness, and it made no sense, because you need an ego to practice any form of art, including translation. Despite these little frictions, Guillermo was a positive influence in my life.

I particularly remember how he encouraged creativity, including my solo translation of a *tour de farce*, as he would say, which one could describe as an impenetrable (and obliquely racist in Cuban mode) flash fiction piece from the book he published right after *TTT*. The book of miscellany which included this brief text was called *Exorcismos de Esti(l)o* (1976) in homage to French surrealist Raymond Queneau's literary acrobatic and famous title which I translated as "Exorcizing a Sty(le)." The piece of resistance in question, which I faithfully titled "The Ides of March According to Plutarch According to Shakespeare According to Joseph Mankiewicz," lands us in the midstream of a confusing monologue about Mark Antony's monologue played by a larger-than-life Marlon Brando. The garrulous speaker I attempt to translate is a shoeshine "boy," who may not know Shakespeare but who has the street smarts to recognize bullshit, is explaining the plot of this corny 1950s film based on *Julius Caesar* to a customer as he shines his shoes.

In Guillermo's spoken Cuban text this monologue is "recorded" exactly, phonetically, as spoken, that is, the music of Cuban Spanish. I had to turn the character's earthy slurred speech into Spanglish with devices that worked in English, devices in African American phrases and pronunciation such as contractions, comic misspellings, misunderstandings (like calling a scroll a roll of toilet paper) or mispronunciations which seem unintentionally creative. Guillermo read my translation with speechless amazement (not typical of him) as he the author, he claimed, could not reconstruct his original rendering of all the ins and outs of the meandering deluge of Cuban speech sounds spilling onto the page. Here is a sampling from the "transcreation":

> Well man the thing is that this guy Ceezer dont wanna be king but he really duz or duznt but he really wants the crown and I dont know whats the big deal … when this guy Brutish comes along who aint so Brutish but who's pretty brutish ….Then comes this guy with a beard and a roll of toilet paper in his hand who's the friend of some fortuneteller who already tol Ceezer what wuz goin to happin to 'im on the Idas or Ideas of March which seems to be a bad month for crazy people and for hares and so on ….[4]

Guillermo could be thorny, but he was also, as mentioned, generous. Even after we no longer were actively collaborating, he urged me, or felt it was important for me to write the literary biography of our mutual friend Manuel Puig. He helped substantially by recalling colorful anecdotes in Puig's life and making available personal letters, but mostly he helped by just "being there"— that is, being a living, lively incarnation of the era and the people I was trying to resurrect. And now Guillermo was among the irreplaceable, as Manuel Puig in 1988 would write to me a heart-felt letter about Emir, missing those exciting hectic times the three of us shared in New Haven in the 1970s.

Like Emir, Guillermo could be a thoughtful and compassionate advisor, as when we were together at a film festival in homage to John Cassavetes in Barcelona in 1989. I was agonizing over a break-up with my second woman partner, Claudia, who had been a childhood chum from Juilliard days and who, when I accepted a teaching position at the University of Washington, miraculously re-entered my life. We had lost track of each other in the 1960s, so in 1984, in our thirties, we were overjoyed to reconnect in Seattle, especially as we still had the same goofy sense of humor that had bonded us back then. The latent eros we no doubt shared as kids quickly blossomed into adult passion.

While we were both humanities professors and shared affinities and experiences, we had parted ways of being on the road from childhood to adulthood. Also, between us the obstacles of geographic distance, so typical in the lives of academics forced to teach far from where their partners live and work, did not help to build closeness and trust. Perhaps the memory of our platonic childhood romance should have been left in its sacred place, though our brief five-year union as adults, especially the first couple of years, did bring us rich and joyful moments. There was a certain magic in having a second chance to be together with our intellects in full regalia as well as our bodies.

Several months after we parted ways, I eventually came to grips with the fact that my misery was, in psychobabble, the aftermath of a "narcissistic blow." During our conversations in Barcelona, Guillermo made an earnest effort to pull me out of my depression; he emphasized that he regretted all the precious time, "three lifetimes" he said, he had wasted on failed romances and he insisted that "In six months, you're not going to give a shit about her, so for God's sake, end it now!" What he said sounded stronger in the original Spanish, of course, by using "mother" as a curse word: "En seis meses te vas a cagar en su madre." How right he was, and I appreciated that he had stepped out of his cynicism to be a comforting confidant.

But before all this happened, many adventures awaited me with Manuel Puig whom I met in the same year (1969) I had met Cabrera Infante, and during the years that followed I translated several works of both writers, almost creating between them a rivalry. Rivalries among writers, and not only Latin Americans, was a commonality I noticed a lot in those years. A famous incident in the 1970s involved a punch in the face delivered by Mario Vargas Llosa, a new young Peruvian writer, to the world-famous Gabriel García Márquez. The apparent reason was that Gabo (García Márquez) had flirted with Mario's pretty wife (and cousin)—but this could have been a political argument as well over Fidel Castro, or even more, an underlying literary rivalry.

5

1970s: The "Buenos Aires Affair" in New York

Puig is a common surname in Spanish, with a Catalan etymology that means "hill" and was pronounced as "pweeg" not as "puch" because, as South Americans, his family used Castilian rather than Catalan pronunciation. The novelist Manuel Puig is remembered today, by people over forty or fifty, mainly because of the Oscar-winning movie and the Broadway musical hit based on his fourth novel, *Kiss of the Spider Woman*. Born in 1932 in a small town on the Argentine pampas, Manuel found his salvation in writing. Growing up as a homosexual in a Catholic country, he had to live a double life, even with his family.

By the time I met Manuel, he was an up-and-coming star (or "starlet" as he always preferred the feminine). *La traición de Rita Hayworth*, his first novel to be published in Spanish, had won a major prize in Spain, and his second novel *Boquitas pintadas* was a bestseller in South America. *Betrayed by Rita Hayworth* began as a failed screenplay—Manuel's driving ambition since childhood had been to make movies—and became his autobiographical first novel. It was not only radically unconventional in its form, in which only the characters speak and there is apparently no author, but also in its content, strongly focused on women, a subversive approach within a patriarchal culture of machismo.

The characters are mostly children, adolescents, and women, and the reader is guided only by what appears to be their unexpurgated monologues or dialogues in which the speakers are not identified. There are also diaries, a written assignment for school, and a letter, and the main character is Toto (thinly disguising Puig's own childhood nickname, Coco), a lonely boy who becomes a keen voyeur of the adult world, so that he is not only one of the speakers but also, like the reader, a listener.

As a translator, I was swept away by Puig's perfectly nuanced, almost uncanny imitations of Argentine voices, distinct according to age, gender or class. As I began to translate this novel it was both exciting and difficult to undertake this creative challenge, to bring into English the living spoken language of the original, to reproduce their natural voice, the way they speak. With his camp sensibility he pinpoints so accurately the kitsch euphemisms, the everyday language of evasion. His books are subtle works of art using campy comically unsubtle materials, accessible yet sophisticated; they had popular appeal but were also high art.

In his many interviews, Manuel explained the role of movies in his childhood, telling us that "Mama would take me to the movies in the afternoons to entertain me and herself, and I decided that reality was what was on the screen and that my fate was to live lost in the middle of the pampas in a bad impromptu Western." The movies that were "reality" to him were Hollywood dreams in the form of melodramas and comedies. His childhood at the movies was an escape from a dreary and limited everyday life in a small rural town.

In Washington Heights, the New York neighborhood where I grew up in the 1950s and early 1960s, when my mother and father took me with them to the movies on Saturday nights as they couldn't afford a babysitter, this excursion was the biggest treat of the week, as it was for Toto in Manuel's novel. My parents seemed oblivious to the impact the more "mature" films might have on a child; I was around twelve (when foreign films were still rare if not taboo) when they took me to *And God Created Woman*. This French film featured the sexiest woman in the world at that time, Brigitte Bardot, who appears in the nude and whose husband might be impotent. Whether or not I was aware of what impotence meant, the film pulsated with perverse eroticism and I felt curious about it but, needless to say, nobody explained anything.

In the monologue of five-year-old Toto in *Betrayed by Rita Hayworth*, Manuel shows how his young avatar was disturbed by a supposedly educational film shown at school about the sea world. As an innocent spectator he thinks the underwater images are "hairy" plants that look like what he seems to consider threatening vaginas swallowing little fish; he associates the hairy image with a sex act he spies on between a boy and a girl, a scene I translated as, "… the boy's hairs start eating her behind … and little by little eats her all up." Sex looks very scary from this perspective for the young child.

Through his first novel, Manuel already seemed to be inviting the reader to understand his homosexuality, or to have, at least, compassion for his plight. I could relate this invitation to my own need to understand and to accept my problematic relationships, with older men and then with gay men, and my association of the erotic with perversion or taboos. I had much older siblings, and in a way, I grew up as an "only" child, on the sidelines of the life of older parents, just as Toto saw movies through his mother's eyes. By sharing intensely his mother's excursions to the movie and that for her, going to the movies was a wondrous escape, the happiest moment of her day, for him the world and the movies became one, and he preferred the movies, a better version of reality. The movies for millions of people during hard times were a way to escape, to liberate themselves from conscious worries, or to will oneself into a better life. Such was the case of my parents, a perspective that I adopted, like Toto, before I was aware that it was a point of view rather than a fact.

When I met him in 1969, Manuel was stopping on his way from Paris to Buenos Aires. Manuel was an incessant traveler, not unusual for an Argentine and, in those days, for a gay man. Argentina, at the bottom of South America, is a country way off course, and populated mostly with the children of Europeans for whom traveling is like breathing, who miss the world, the centers of culture, so very far way. Manuel always claimed to be seeking true love, and I do believe he was. Mexico and New York would be home in exile from fascist Argentina until he moved to Brazil in 1980, however, he constantly traveled in pursuit of his profession and, as he said, true love, often at bookfairs, where he would meet with publishers and translators. Like most Argentines who had the means to travel, he felt isolated in his home country not only because of its hostility to homosexuals, but because it was so far from Gotham and Paris, or 42nd Street and the Moulin Rouge, that is, civilization.

He was good-looking, like an Italian version of Tyrone Power, my partner Emir had told me, and so when I saw a slight, dark-haired fellow who vaguely fit this La Dolce Vita description briskly enter the revolving door of the Chinese restaurant in Greenwich Village that cold night in December, I knew it had to be Puig. His neck wrapped in a scarf up to his nose, and wearing a leather jacket, he quickly sighted Emir and came over to our booth. I could tell from Manuel's big mischievous eyes with long thick eyelashes, that he was surprised upon meeting me, perhaps slightly shocked by the age gap, having known his distinguished friend Emir (who looked his years at forty-eight) as the husband of an elegant Uruguayan society woman his own age, and here he was with this American girl with straight brown hair and bangs, who looked so young. Manuel took in this contrast with one writerly glance as the two of them chatted eagerly, catching up, not having seen each other for quite some time, with a lot of water under the bridge for them both. I chimed in now and again, especially when the subject was movies.

Figure 5.1 Jill and Manuel Puig in Buenos Aires bookstore, September 1971. (Photo credit: *Gente.*)

Manuel—for whom the last great Hollywood film was *Sunset Boulevard*, made in 1950—found the "new realism" of contemporary films to be limited and limiting. Hence, he nicknamed four "new Hollywood" (i.e., real rather than glamorous) 1970s women stars (among them the admirable Ellen Burstyn) the "Four Horsewomen of the Apocalypse." This was not a compliment. However, despite differing opinions, from the very beginning of our now shared friendship with Manuel, Emir and I participated in playful cinematic complicity with Manuel who renamed us, as he did all his friends, as film stars. Emir was George Brent, a "mildly sinister" (Manuel's words) romantic lead in the 1940s, now completely forgotten but famous for the melodramas he made with Bette Davis. These comparisons of his friends with movie stars were funny exaggerations but also accurate portraits.[5]

In our correspondence to each other about the translations, he sometimes addressed me as "Dear Silvana" (Silvana Mangano) a very flattering nom de plume as she was an exquisite bombshell in the Italian cinema, known for her scantily dressed role in the neorealist award-winning film *Bitter Rice*. For

Manuel, the roles actors played or, shall we say, the inhabitants of movies, were as real as real people. When I first saw Woody Allen's *The Purple Rose of Cairo*, in which a character steps off the screen into a lonely spectator's life, I thought for sure that he had "borrowed" the idea from Manuel Puig or maybe even Bioy Casares's 1940 masterpiece *The Invention of Morel* in which a mad scientist captures real-life people in an eternally returning sequence of three-dimensional holograph images, as seen by the startled protagonist.

At that first dinner with Manuel, we discussed how difficult it was to find a translator for *Betrayed by Rita Hayworth*, which Dutton had just accepted for publication. The publisher of new editions of Borges's stories, Jack Macrae III, wanted to hire the bigshot translator Norman Thomas di Giovanni, whose father had named him after the socialist Norman Thomas, six-time presidential candidate for the U.S. Socialist Party. Di Gi spoke like a Boston or Dorchester mafioso and even banged his fist on the table for emphasis. He had convinced Borges and Jack Macrae that he would make Borges a bestseller or at least a more accessible writer for a broader reading public—which he did succeed in doing, as with "Streetcorner Man," Borges's early gangster story "El hombre de la esquina rosada" (literally "the man on the pink corner"). But Di Gi vacillated when they asked him to take on Manuel's *La traición de Rita Hayworth*.

While homophobia might have been a factor, Di Gi claimed that this novel, by an unknown writer, was too dense to hold the interest of readers. He was understandably afraid to damage his reputation if he ran into trouble with Manuel's extensive monologues filled with untranslatable slang and local Argentine speech mannerisms. And he was right: what the hell to do with those lengthy sentences? This clearly shows how difficult *Rita* was, if you consider that Di Gi knew Spanish like a native and, living in Buenos Aires to be close to Borges, he was totally immersed in the culture. On the other hand, Borges was an exception already in terms of international fame, hence fanning Di Gi's entrepreneurial goals, while, at the time, the writers I chose to translate, or was chosen for, were unknown, like myself, and were probably not for large audiences.

Betrayed by Rita Hayworth—as well as *Three Trapped Tigers*—was described as a "gallery of voices." I had already collaborated with Guillermo Cabrera Infante on the untranslatable *cubanismos* of *TTT* and both Emir and Manuel had recommended me to Jack Macrae III. The fact that I had the support of Emir, a Yale professor who was writing a literary biography of Borges for Dutton, helped convince Jack, who became a good friend over the years, and who, like so many from those days, is no longer with us. Among his many literary achievements, while still living in Uruguay, Emir had translated Shakespeare's *Twelfth Night* into Spanish for a theater production in collaboration with a prominent poet, Idea Vilariño. As one who appreciated the literary value and art of translation, Emir was an enormous support.

Translating the title of Manuel's second novel *Boquitas pintadas* ("little painted lips") which had just come out in 1969, was yet another Mount Everest of translation. The key difficulty was to recreate for the English language reader the tension between irony and sentimentality in the original lyrics of the title song, words well-known to his contemporary Argentine readers as they had been popularized by the country's most famous crooner of tangos, Carlos Gardel. The dark sexuality of the tango words and dance moves was a melodramatic cliché associated with the theme of passion and love lost. After translating, with varied success, Argentine tango lyrics cited in the novel, we came up with the word "heartbreak" as an emotional equivalent in English, and hence the title *Heartbreak Tango*, which eventually struck us—author, translator and editor—as a plausible title.

For the dialogues we had Hollywood "women's pictures," as many 1940s films were called, and I also could consult my sister Alice, who was from an older generation, to help me come up with kitschy language. Finding the language to reiterate similar absurd bureaucratic formalities and song lyrics required a good ear in English, and Manuel as collaborator provided a short cut to finding germane substitutions. Translating his novel meant discovering how to say something so natural when the closest words, images and syntax in Spanish would look so different.

Where, for instance, a pre-Second World War cliché like "estoy tan caida," literally "I am so (fallen) down," I needed to stress the pathetic, hence I chose, "I'm feeling so down in the mouth"—a sad utterance but striking a comic note of "kitchen sink" exaggeration for the reader.[6] The tango lyrics in the stream of consciousness of certain characters infuse the novel's atmosphere, as does "down in the mouth," which visually and rhythmically emphasizes the tango's typical falling motion in which the dancers mimic the act of falling. While the literal "fallen" for "caida" wouldn't work in the woman's sad yet kitschy complaint, "down" is a clear example of how translation works metonymically, that is, by following associated or closely related images.

It would never be totally the same or the "real" thing, but the puzzle-solving to seek ways to recreate the humor was, again, an intriguing undertaking. In

Heartbreak the reader at first chuckles at the characters because they are run-of-the-mill men and woman in traditional roles, and readers thus can identify with their fatal flaws. Manuel's characters make mistakes like most of us in the arenas of career and love, but by the same token, the novel seduces the reader into caring about these "ordinary people," whose lives fall short of their aspirations.

To be absurd is to be human, but what was very different from any other (male) writer in the 1970s was Puig's singular grasp of the thoughts and feelings of his women characters whose words, after all, were his. With his agile capacity for narrative invention, his writerly bisexuality rang true to my own sense of being "neither fish nor fowl" as, in the past, my brother had gently provoked me. Humor is an indirect way to tell a truth not easily accepted, and while I enjoyed any attention my older siblings gave me, I could also feel the sting.

*

In the third Puig novel, published in Spanish with an English title *The Buenos Aires Affair*—Manuel did this mainly to facilitate its translation into English—there is an imagined interview of Gladys, Manuel Puig's female avatar, while she is lying in bed with Leo her virile lover. At this point in the story, Gladys feels that finally after much frustration, she is not only being recognized as an artist but is also under the illusion that she has discovered true love. What she experiences as true love, however, the reader experiences as delusional, as corny melodrama.

> Reporter: "… you have become a star in the art world. Do you believe that you have now achieved your highest ambition?"
>
> Gladys: "No, my highest ambition is to be a woman who finds fulfillment in her love life, and, what a paradox, in my case career has led me to love."[7]

Fiction and life went hand in hand when it came to love and melodrama, for the reader as well as the writer. While it did not always feel like a "labor of love," translating Puig afforded a certain pleasure, like solving a puzzle, more a labor of fun. Like all creative writing, translating Puig emerged out of a libidinal or "intimate" connection to the written page, and so could be what Roland Barthes famously called "the pleasure of the text." This phrase pertained to Barthes's reading of Severo Sarduy's neo-baroque novel *Cobra*, a hallucinatory text which, like the bodies of its characters, undergoes a series of metamorphoses, and which I was translating in the same period.

To give the Dutton editors a sense of Manuel's first novel and the translation, I chose a sample of the "authentic" language in the novel, the monologue of a delinquent high school kid—the only Jewish character in the novel, named Cobito (short for Jacobo)—who threatens to rape the "sissy" Toto in the school locker room. Manuel explained in an interview that he thought this character would appeal to his Jewish friends because Jews were normally not depicted as machos but rather as nerdy bookworms. Cobito's monologue was thorny as well as horny and starts with, "I'm going to murder those bastards," rapidly moving onto violent sexual acts or fantasies in language like, "I'll make mincemeat out of you, you bitch." Still kind of a kid myself at twenty-three, I liked coming up with the curse words that fit the bill, and also that the bad boy was Jewish, but I also reasoned that the boy's monologue, while dense with pent-up fury, would deliver the sexuality and violence of a colorful local slang and therefore could appeal to a broad audience—beginning with the editor at Dutton. The erotic passages were an incentive to shoulder the laborious prospect of unraveling monologues that sometimes lasted a whole page or more, the game of finding the words and phrasing to convey Cobito's verbal assaults.

I wrote to Manuel the day I delivered the finished manuscript to Dutton, and before long an exuberant, typically hyperbolic letter from "Rita" arrived, addressing me with Argentine exaggerations such as "divine one": "Divina: Thank you immensely for your talent! I'm thrilled to the bones!!!" My early success as a translator was exhilarating, and the friendships that blossomed were inseparable from the thrill of the work itself. In the languages Manuel knew well, French, Italian, English and even German, Manuel tended to treat his translators with kid gloves, as did Guillermo Cabrera Infante often with mischievous humor. Connecting with the translator smoothed the way for both these postmodern authors to engage in recreating the book for new readers.

As the young translator of such a daring book as *Rita Hayworth*, I was generously recognized by the *New York Times*. Thanks to John A. Coleman's gushing review which came out prominently with a sexy full-page image of the actress Rita Hayworth in the Sunday Book Review in 1971, our translation was described as "full of literary allure!" The review's humorous language is infused with John Coleman's first meeting with Manuel who, an incorrigible man-chaser, tried to seduce him. When we introduced John and Manuel a year earlier, Manuel slightly terrified John Coleman with what Coleman defines in the novel as "magnetic glower, smoldering good looks, panache and plenty of strut!" This seemed to be the only explanation for John's hasty retreat to the exit of the Center where we had all gathered: after a few drinks he attempted to slide down a curving banister and, terrifying us all, lost his balance and fell almost thirty feet upon the marble floor below, an accident which cost him months in a body cast. Manuel Puig, in any case, was now launched in New York, and with translations proliferating in France, Italy and Japan, onto the world market as the greatest Argentine literary discovery since Borges and Cortázar—and I made my critical debut as translator of one of Latin America's most exciting new writers.

*

Manuel Puig landed in New York for the first time in February of 1963, the month my mother would have turned fifty-seven but had died that January 1st. He was completely in awe when he finally saw in real time the skyscrapers which he had seen on the silver screen. Having visited New York in the movies since childhood, he was moved to describe the dazzling "beauty and poetry" of those steel towers in his first letter from "Gotham" to his intimate confidant Mario Fenelli, another Argentine movie queen adrift in Cinecitta.

The two young men had met as film students together in Rome—a city Manuel considered provincial compared to Paris and New York. Another student friend at the film school in Rome, an exiled Cuban whose parents in turn had been exiles from Spain to Cuba after Franco became dictator in 1939, was the young cinematographer Nestor Almendros who would become world-famous, winning an Oscar for *Days of Heaven* (1978) and two more nominations: *Kramer vs Kramer* (1979) and *Sophie's Choice* (1982). In that first letter from New York to Mario, Manuel spoke of himself as he commonly did, in the third person feminine, with a nickname "Sally" given to him by Nestor. Sally was inspired in part by Christopher Isherwood's "Sally" as well as a character played in *The Strawberry Blonde* by stunning red-headed film star Rita Hayworth. Manuel was also "Rita" especially during the time that novel appeared. The nostalgia and sharp critique that intermingle in Manuel's novels and other writings, also pepper this personal letter to Mario Fenelli of 1963:

> Sally writes to you from the land where she went to look for a husband. Will she find him? ... Where to begin? ... The people here seem straight out of Dickens. Those exaggerated toughs from the Damon Runyon movies are no exaggeration ...

Upon his arrival that February, the airport bus had left him and a huge suitcase on 42nd Street in the sleazy heart of midtown, and he expressed his terror to Mario that the streets were "teeming with fags, blacks and Central Americans!" Damon Runyon was a Depression-era New York newspaperman. His entertaining stories like "Guys and Dolls" were made into gangster movies with comedic characters who spoke in tough-guy regional slang, movies we all watched in those days. My father sometimes sounded (or at least this is what I remember) like those characters, dropping the "h" in "thirty" and changing "ir" to "oi"—as in "toity-toid street and toid avenue."

In those years, until Times Square was renovated in the 1990s, 42nd Street looked nothing like the futuristic cyber circus of today but was rather a broad littered rundown street of sleazy bars and third-rate movie theaters whose marquees announced porn or horror films. Carrying that heavy suitcase, Manuel had to walk a few blocks to his destination, the nearest YMCA. He was finally in Gotham, the city he had dreamed of for years. Seeking sex which he referred to as romance, he was not one to stay away from baths and alleyways, so it is not surprising that, enjoying the freedoms of the city, he ran across a few "Damon Runyon" types. After an exciting though brief stay at the YMCA, a fount of erotic encounters, he found a roommate who had an apartment way uptown which he could share, on 155th St. and Riverside Drive, the southern border of Washington Heights. This was a mere forty blocks south of 192nd St. and Broadway where I, a high school student, was still residing that winter.

This peripheral zone of the city provided unexpected perks for Manuel, such as art deco movie palaces where "the projection is impeccable." Those grand old theaters from the 1930s showed double bills for only 75 cents to $1.25, and Manuel would arrange his weekly fix by attending Wednesday matinees of Broadway plays and musicals when the orchestra tickets cost only four to five dollars. My parents and I had probably attended the same double bills, and there was one theater on 181st St. that showed three films: you'd be dizzy by the time you staggered out of the theater in time for dinner.

The format of multiple films in one show faded out eventually and by the late 1960s, even those more "popular" movie houses were featuring just one film at a time. While I would not meet Manuel for another six years, in 1963 we could have passed each other on a street or sat in the same theater such as the Loew's movie palace on 175th St., where the projection was indeed impeccable.

Around the same time, to survive in Gotham, Manuel Puig had found a job at the VIP desk for Air France. At the counter where he sat and worked every day on the novel that would become "Rita Hayworth," he got to see in person, on their way to or from Europe or Hollywood, celebrities including movie legends such as Greta Garbo and Alfred Hitchcock. Manuel could do such a perfect imitation of Greta Garbo's Swedish accent and every gesture, that after seeing and hearing him play her role as the ballerina in *Grand Hotel* who falls in love with a dashing baron played by an alcoholic John Barrymore, it was not hard to imagine that Greta Garbo was the mimic imitating Manuel's imitation of Greta Garbo, "I want to be alone."

*

Early in his literary career Manuel answered interviews by inventing an anti-literary persona and often joked with his friends that "I'm only a simple woman." He refused critical jargon and would claim that he was unable to write in "normal" Spanish or what was thought of as educated Spanish. By letting his characters do the talking and even writing, they could make the mistakes he claimed he was afraid of making. While there was truth in this expressed insecurity about writing and especially public speaking, no doubt exacerbated by homophobia in the culture around him, the point of this "act" was that he was trying to incorporate a new vision of art in his writing. One critic accurately defined him as Latin America's first "pop art" novelist.

I watched him deliver such a response to John Barth, a celebrated "experimental" American novelist who wrote an influential essay motivated by his discovery of Borges, defining literary postmodernism as the "Literature of Exhaustion." Barth asked Manuel why he chose to revive the epistolary novel in his second work, *Heartbreak Tango*, which Manuel and I were presenting in 1974 at Johns Hopkins University. Barth had just published and was receiving at that time a shower of praise for his novel *LETTERS*. He was a tall academic yet pleasant looking man in glasses and approached Manuel explaining that he was excited about working with the genre of the epistolary novel that had been out of favor in recent times, but which had been so fashionable and such an effective invention in the eighteenth century. Manuel listened respectfully with his big eyes beaming at Barth. Barth eagerly awaited an intriguing explanation but was abruptly deflated; without any hint of high motives, Manuel gave the "simple" woman answer that, to avoid grammatical mistakes, he had his characters write letters in his novel. This way the reader would know the author was not to blame for the (intentional) misspellings or grammatical mistakes.

Barth nodded speechlessly. This humble and ultimately mischievous response was not what he expected, so he spent the next few minutes chatting amiably, while trying to figure out how such an original writer could be so modest or maybe this behavior was Latin American? Or maybe Manuel was pulling his leg? One can only hope that Barth eventually figured out that clever Puig was replaying in new clothes the oldest trick in novel writing, taking a leaf out of Cervantes who claimed in his preface to *Don Quixote*, that the book was a manuscript some Arab fellow had given him and that he had simply translated it into Spanish.

The exchange with Barth was typical; Manuel caught people off-guard because underneath his reputation as a respected Argentine writer there was another identity, perhaps more authentic and certainly less acceptable. The identity or persona as a campy queen that Manuel adopted or as a simple Argentine girl who was unsure of how to write well in proper Spanish, was puzzling to a "serious" writer like Barth—or like Roland Barthes when his friend Severo Sarduy introduced Manuel his "sister" to the French intellectual in Paris.

Through movies, as Manuel was always saying, he discovered who he wanted to be. He didn't desire Greta Garbo: he desired to be her. He was "Greta" the Great Garbo or "Rita" the nickname he gave the first novel, or "Sally" again like Sally Bowles in Isherwood's 1930s *Goodbye to Berlin*, immortalized by Liza Minelli in *Cabaret*. Manuel drew his friends onto the screen with him, naming us after stars, mostly actresses, as I mentioned earlier, according to the occasion, as when he called me "Silvana" after Silvana Mangano, which of course flattered and delighted me enormously as a movie addict.

After the Chinese dinner the night I first met Manuel with Emir, the three of us, enthused to continue our time together in New York went to see, the next afternoon, a movie both wished to revisit and which I would see for the first time. There was a special showing at the Film and Cultural Center located at Columbus Circle on 59th street; the building itself was worth the visit, an odd "modernist" beehive-looking structure. The movie was a classic from Hollywood of course, the screwball comedy *Nothing Sacred*, a satire of journalism about a cynical New York newspaperman and a small-town girl played by the talented Carole Lombard, who tragically would die young in an airplane accident during the Second World War.

The film was directed by Ben Hecht in 1937, and starred Fredric March, another of Manuel's favorite performers. Some of his choices I agreed with, but others were mystifying, like Fredric March. Throughout this hilarious film Manuel never laughed—which had me mystified—but sat silently transfixed with those big expressive eyes as if recording every detail. Meanwhile the appreciative audience laughed raucously at the rapid-fire dialogue and slapstick shenanigans.

This incident was typical, again, of Manuel's bullet-proof knack for catching people off-guard. During a transitional nightclub scene when the audience was silent, the svelte, glamorous and inebriated Lombard stands up, daintily tottering. Like the rest of the audience, Emir and I quietly awaited the next wisecrack, when suddenly, out of the dark abyss, we were stunned by a loud exclamation, high-pitched from Manuel, sitting next to us: "¡Ay, qué traje divino!" (What a gorgeous dress!). Manuel was merely emoting over how beautiful the actress looked in a shimmering silk gown, thus uttering "divino," a campy cliché from his mother's lexicon. When I met her, I immediately saw that Manuel's model was his mother and that he internalized whatever she said or did when as a child he accompanied her to movies. Nestor Almendros wasn't joking when he said the real Manuel Puig was his mother Malé Puig.

*

By 1973, the political environment in Argentina was perilous and, after *The Buenos Aires Affair* was censored because of its taboo or profane treatment of sexuality in the "sacred" context of Peronism, Manuel's life was threatened by a right-wing terrorist group. The tireless traveler, he left Buenos Aires and moved to New York. He would never return to Argentina. He was fleeing not only the fascist politics reflected in the "critical" eye toward him as a gay man, but also the envy or jealousy of fellow writers. *The Buenos Aires Affair*, disguised as a detective novel, portrays such rivalries by creating the sado-masochistic affair between a male art critic and a female artist. The book disappointed many readers of the two previous novels I had translated but, in retrospect, it would be valued by local intellectuals as the most acute dissection of fascism in Argentina's cultural politics during the 1970s by an Argentine novelist.

Manuel and I had plans to work on the next translation for Dutton as soon as he settled in New York, and so he arrived on a snowy night in January 1974, again in the northern hemisphere's winter. Now in graduate school, I was renting a room in a corner apartment on King St. for the two or three nights a week I went to the city to attend classes at NYU. With the permission of my New York roommate Merle Kaufman, whose two-bedroom apartment it was, I had invited Manuel to stay there for a week or so until he found his own digs. A zoftig woman my age, Merle earned her keep as a therapist and, in a glass cage, kept a pet iguana named Geraldo Rivera after the TV "personality" of whom she was enamored. She was quite charmed to meet Manuel, which often happened with women who found him attractive, sometimes to his dismay. He was especially uncomfortable if pursued by mature women, which meant his own age or older. "Too motherly," he said as if it were taboo, or perhaps, "too much like mother," whereas girls or young women were fair game.

As suggested earlier, I was beginning to recognize my own bisexual tendencies, about which I believe that my brother and parents may have had unspoken hunches in my childhood. But didn't every spectator, man or woman, adopt the male gaze at the reified figures of sex goddesses? At the movies as a youngster, I was attracted to the finely chiseled features of Gregory Peck and the perfectly gorgeous French actor Alain Delon, but with equal intensity I loved gazing at super sexy Elizabeth Taylor and Gina Lollobrigida. As an adult, it is not surprising, whether rejecting heterosexuality or dealing with depression, that I was drawn to like-minded acquaintances who were usually gay, people with whom I could be free to subvert the pessimism of feeling like an outsider.

My extravagant gay friend, the writer Bruce Benderson—and in whom I confided, more than any other friend, about my intimate problems—was the first to suggest that I should explore women. Bruce initially thought of me as totally femme and we playfully flirted, mainly with campy irony, but when I drove us both in the car I used to commute between New Haven and the city, he was surprised by my aggressive driving, as it were a shocking revelation. For me (also for my sister Alice as she once told me) driving a car felt liberating, so perhaps one could say I was liberating the male side of myself. Driving a car was, in a sense, one way a female could participate as an equal in a male world.

Originally from the solid middle-class suburbia of Syracuse, New York, Bruce had fled to New York City from gay mecca San Francisco because it was "cold and damp"—which was one motive for the song made famous by Frank Sinatra, "The Lady is a Tramp." Eager to break into the East Village literary world, Bruce cultivated a writerly community that included offbeat strong-willed women like Ursule Molinaro, Eileen Myles and especially his college buddy, the notorious Camille Paglia. She and Bruce knew each other from Harpur College—the artsy intellectual branch of SUNY Binghamton. When Bruce first introduced me to Camille, she seemed shy or mousy, and she was plump before blossoming into a vampish cult figure, becoming a wiry cat-woman engaged in the embattled realm of sexual politics. He and Camille were often bickering, Bruce would report over the years, sparring intellectual contrarians, and somewhere in the '90s parted ways over one bicker too many.

Not yet the novelist and cultural critic he was to become, Bruce Benderson was just starting out as a French translator and we hit it off right away. I met Bruce in the sweltering heat of Paris in August, 1973 with Severo Sarduy, a Cuban "loca" (as he described himself) exiled in Paris who seemed more like a rhumba dancer than the neo-baroque novelist, postmodern essayist and avant-garde "textual" painter that he was. I had just translated a chapter of *Cobra* that had appeared in a journal. Severo's playful complex texts, threaded with hip multi-cultural references from "pop" to arcane, had many layers, and Severo was glad to enlighten me when I consulted him.

That August I was looking for a place to stay in Paris and the brilliant impish Severo, already a chum of mine, on this occasion was introducing me to a fellow Cuban as well as Jewish friend, the erudite fine arts scholar David Bigelman. David and Bruce were friends since meeting in the gay mecca of San Francisco, hence Bruce was at the luncheon David graciously served in his studio apartment, and thus began our friendship. David generously loaned me his pied-à-terre for my few days in Paris as it was August and he, a professor at L'Ecole des Beaux Arts, was leaving on vacation.

David was an erudite art and architecture connoisseur as well as generous host over the next years in Paris, and we'd often go to art shows or tour around the city together. I stayed another time with him in the 1980s when he had a more luxurious apartment near the National Library. And then one day I learned, sadly, that he died of AIDS in 2003, ten years after Severo Sarduy died of that terrible plague.

Bruce and I reconnected in New York that fall 1973. Emir, with his world of writers, artists and intellectuals from Latin America and beyond, was a cherished being in my life. But Bruce was not only fun but a peer and I missed companions my own age and from my own milieu, whatever that was by then. While I loved Emir, the romantic intensity had faded, and conflictive feelings gnawed at me. It was as if, throughout my twenties, I hadn't allowed myself enough space and time when I possessed it, to enjoy my youth. Water under the bridge, my predicament shared a sense of loss with those child actors who, like Natalie Wood, worked so hard that they didn't get to live fully their childhood. For me this all was complicated by an ambivalence that, in some ways, has never left me: being a translator was a creative way to deal with ambivalence, with one's "fluidity," a better term for bisexuality, less categorical, more experiential. What I mean is, a translator is constantly resolving or reconciling the problem of how two languages are not the same, do not match each other perfectly and yet the art of translating meant finding ways to resolve ambivalence, at least on the written page. And with gay men, I could sidestep the obstacle of ambivalence, turn it into subversive irreverence.

I introduced Bruce to Manuel that winter of 1974, and they quickly embraced a campy bond as fellow parishioners of seedy New York gay life in that era. During the years after Manuel left New York, when he was living in Brazil in the 1980s and would visit New York on business, he usually stayed at Bruce's East Village pad on St. Marks near 2nd avenue. Bruce, tall and gangly with his quirky smarts, then lived directly across the street from the historic St. Marks theater, a treasure trove of foreign, avant-garde and Hollywood classic cinema which the two "sisters" would often attend together to visit their favorite divas on screen.

Bruce was a confidant in those agitated mid-1970s when Emir and I were often in a sad limbo, that is, in the unhappy process of splitting up. I wanted freedom to do whatever crossed my path, and yet to follow this path I knew I would have to give up the only person who was there for me, with whom I had a deep-felt emotional connection. During this time, I met through Bruce an interesting young woman who looked like she belonged in the 1950s, Kay Agena, a freelance editor. Kay worked for not enough to live on, and freelanced mainly for the *Partisan Review*, a highly respected cultural journal at that time, founded by two left-wing Jewish editors.

As she lived on King Street too, we became pals; books, movies, love life, our projects and the ups and downs of literary life were our constant topics. At some point Kay had had a flirtation (probably more) with the elderly roué who was the journal's co-founder and senior editor—though the unavailable man with whom she was having an ongoing sporadic affair was a burly young novelist. Our conversations and laughs over misery allowed us to let off steam about the sufferings of love or achieving stability.

Anyway, during our months with Manuel in the mid-1970s, Kay lived half a block west from Merle's on King Street, the very same block where Elizabeth Bishop had once lived. Merle's apartment was too crowded for three occupants and so Kay generously, for a modest contribution to help cover her rent, offered Manuel temporary lodgings in her walk-up brownstone flat. He was her roommate for a week or two until he was offered an apartment all to himself, thanks to an Argentine friend Norberto Gonzalez, who would be away in Buenos Aires until early fall.

A midwestern highbrow adrift in New York, Kay had a curious combination of subtle wit and sincerity. Physically a blue-eyed curly blonde with a 1950s hairdo, she reminded Manuel and Bruce of Hope Lang, a 1950s Hollywood actress, blonde and blue-eyed, who often played sincere roles, as in *Peyton Place*, an iconic film of that repressive era. Kay was an oddball Village bohemian in the way she dressed and in her quiet gentility. Her Greek surname Agena, close to Agony, seemed apropos even though, despite her quiet melancholy, she was also an optimist. Always the sharp-edged observer of people, Manuel cast Kay, with her ethereal aura, in the role of a nun one evening, to entertain Bruce and myself when the two of them invited us over to Kay's cozy apartment where they lit candles, covered their heads in shawls, knelt piously and prayed, and recited church words like "pro nobis" in ersatz Latin.

Occasionally Bruce, Kay and I would manage to convince Manuel to join us for dinner. I remember one icy January evening in 1974 we were all at a nearby Japanese restaurant on Sixth or Seventh Avenue that was inexpensive and modestly arranged with wooden booths. Kay, Bruce and I were talking and at times jesting animatedly about a movie or boyfriends or recent news, but Manuel seemed strangely absent. After a while he finally emerged from what seemed a dream state and uttered two words, "La Hedy" and sighed. All during dinner, apparently, he had been focused on the exquisitely beautiful actress Hedy Lamarr, the central figure in *Pubis Angelical*, the novel he was writing at that moment.

In the 1940s Hedy Lamarr, an Austrian-born actress, was considered one of the most beautiful faces in Hollywood, with chiseled features and irresistible eyes. Unknown at that time was that she was Jewish and, more amazing, was a brilliant code breaker who contributed to the defeat of the Nazis in the Second World War. She had managed to escape extermination by the Third Reich and, unhappily, a mystery woman in real life, she died in abject poverty. The Hedy Lamarr movie *The Strange Woman* made in 1946 (my birth year) was perhaps the film Manuel identified most with, perhaps because he could safely say that he too was a strange woman.

All this felt relevant to me too, as, if you'll remember, my mother had been nicknamed after this film as "the strange woman" by her youngest sister Gertie, my favorite aunt, because my mother was mysterious in that she always kept her grievances to herself, hence "the strange woman." This was my impression, and now in my mature years I realize that I have followed in her untraceable footsteps, except that the one who is mystified is me. In any case I never really knew, though I sometimes worried about what secrets or sorrows my enigmatic mother had on her mind. By the time I was twelve or thirteen, I finally figured out that she often seemed preoccupied. Thinking about it now, I am sure my sister Carol was on Mom's mind. I later learned that mother told my aunt: "She comes home, I put her back together, and she goes back there only to fall apart again." More than strange Mother should have been called "the troubled woman." In any case no one was as strange a woman as Manuel that evening, not only because he was not a woman but because his presence seemed so absent.

By the time winter that year with its slushy dirty snow on the streets was sliding into spring, Manuel was living in his Argentine friend Norberto's apartment at 21 West 58th St., glamorously around the corner from the Plaza Hotel on Fifth Avenue. Manuel had this lovely place to himself, a situation he preferred so that he wouldn't disturb anyone if he wanted to watch a movie on TV at 3:00 a.m. Norberto's well-located art deco building, and especially his apartment, was the well-appointed setting where we worked intensely for a month, usually two afternoons each week, going over the translation of *The Buenos Aires Affair*. Our concentration, however, was not limited to the translation.

During 1970–71 we had corresponded almost every day, and when he was in New York he'd come up to New Haven as a guest speaker at Yale, where we would celebrate his visit with our interesting and attractive New Haven friends, Alfred and Barbara MacAdam. We three—Emir, Manuel and I—even played house in the sense that Manuel would stay over in our guest room, I would cook, and Emir and Manuel would wash and dry the dishes. Emir was called the Uruguayan maid and Manuel the Argentinian maid. It was unnecessary to name me, though "Teresita," a nickname Manuel used sometimes for me to suggest "simple peasant girl," would have worked. Emir was more at ease about gays than almost any other straight man I knew in those days.

Emir and I flew to Paris and London in January 1970, looking forward to great theater and to enjoying the London caravansary of Emir's amusing friends, while Guillermo and I were going over the galleys of *TTT* in London. Along with spending time in London with Guillermo and Miriam, we were joined by Manuel who was there dealing with British publishers. Perhaps the best bit of the London trip was the premiere of two short plays by Harold Pinter—a major event, though minor plays.

In the theater lobby, Manuel and I arrived before the arrival of Emir and the Cabrera Infantes, coming in another cab. As it was too cold to wait outside, we huddled inside the small lobby and, as celebrities made their entrance one by one, Manuel whispered to me, "Let's move over to the wall." Inches away from us, none other than the exquisite French actress Delphine Seyrig (recently in

Buñuel's famous film *The Discreet Charms of the Bourgeoisie*) made her entrance elegantly on the arm of the equally famous English character actor Donald Pleasance; these two were evidently close colleagues or friends. Gazing ecstatically at the graceful Delphine, Manuel exclaimed, "Divine!"

A few minutes later, a tall attractive man with an equally well-attired male companion strolled by us: Edward Albee, Manuel replied to my query, and before I could whisper anything further, Manuel muttered, "That lucky bitch!" His point was that Albee's eminent reputation exceeded his actual talent. Manuel criticized *Who's Afraid of Virginia Woolf* because the heterosexual couple at the center of the drama didn't make sense: for some strange reason they couldn't have a son? They were obviously a disguise for a gay couple, hence for Manuel the play was cowardly or dishonest.

Having seen during my college years the Mike Nichols's film, I quietly disagreed: the work had struck me as daringly original, brilliant with powerful performances by Elizabeth Taylor, her husband the extraordinary Richard Burton, Sandy Dennis, a true original, and the dependable George Segal as the young hunk. I concluded that Manuel, like Proust, had played a similar ruse on readers, for example, in his first three novels. One could argue that, for example, the masochist Gladys and the sadist Leo in *The Buenos Aires Affair* were more like two men than a man and a woman. Perhaps Albee's "cop-out" was too close for comfort?

*

How and where did my first lesbian relationship begin? I am speaking of what happened between myself and Manuel in 1971, not later developments. From the get-go we had been like giggly high school girlfriends together and in our letters strewn with campy nicknames—and even if I desired something more, until then I had thought our flirtation was non-referential, a term in vogue then. I was attracted to Manuel but presumed that this was of little interest to him and that our playful interactions were just a game we played. Emir would always consider us girlfriends, and Manuel once said, "Even if he would have seen us in bed together, he wouldn't have believed it!"

One could flirt with a gay man and not be guilty of infidelity I reasoned, and of course, in certain circles, this had been a common social practice for women (often labeled unpleasantly as fag hags) for generations. But it wasn't until almost two years later, in Buenos Aires, when *Betrayed by Rita Hayworth* was about to come out in 1971, that Manuel revealed to me a side of himself which I didn't believe existed—even though he had confessed to me once that he got a girl pregnant after a secretive shipboard romance on his return voyage to Argentina from Italy around 1960, making love every night, hiding inside rolls of ropes on deck. Despite the impossibility of abortions at that time and the headaches such a mistake caused, Manuel's family felt with relief that there was some hope for Manuel to be "normal."

Sex should be considered merely part of the vegetative life, Manuel said in interviews, contrary to the procreative teachings of the Good Book. Sex was like eating and sleeping, a basic need. "For me the only natural sexuality is total sexuality, with a person of your own gender, with a person of the opposite gender, with an animal, with a plant, with anything."[8] His point here had been iterated by others before him, of course: notably the French writer and demimonde Colette's lesson to her readers that sex should not be confused with the complex emotion of love. Love and affection were deep feelings for someone else that could last a lifetime, but eros was about "the flesh is fresh," a rhyme in English Manuel proclaimed during one of our intimate moments. I felt the truth in this, but it also went against the morality one had learned, more or less, since childhood.

The summer of 1971, as I mentioned earlier, Emir and I went to Brazil and Argentina, where it was a mild winter. It was sometime during our stay in Buenos Aires, when we were in a taxicab, just leaving a tango bar in the famous Boca district where we had been dancing with Manuel and a merry group of friends including Marta Fernandez. Manuel and I were in the back seat, Emir up front, and as usual lively chatter ensued. Suddenly a thigh was against mine and a hand was on my right hand, guiding it to said thigh and beyond: if this had been a cartoon, there would have been two exclamation points in the bubble over my head.

There were no further carnal innuendos until Manuel's arrival in New York that wintry night in 1974. A few weeks later, Manuel and I went for a drink with two attractive classmates of mine (all three of us would become university professors) one late afternoon. A tall athletic-looking Spaniard with imposing aplomb named Gonzalo Diaz-Migoyo, and Ana Maria Gonzalez, a slim, smart, spritely Spanish girl, and I were all attending Juan Goytisolo's class on Maria de Zayas, seventeenth-century nuns and pornography, which was an exciting innovation for the NYU Spanish and Portuguese Department. Goytisolo was one of Spain's most important "experimental" writers, considered an honorable member of the Latin American Boom; he and Emir had a solid literary and personal friendship, and Juan kindly adopted me as well. A memorable moment

Figure 5.2 Jill and Manuel in Lydia's apartment, 1979, New York City. (Photo credit: Lydia Rubio.)

with Juan Goytisolo was the long-awaited death of Franco in 1975. With Juan's intimate friend Barbara Probst Solomon in her Central Park West apartment, we were celebrating, and Juan, normally low key, was exuberant as we drank toast after toast. A somber fellow despite his risqué course, Juan was directing my classmate Ana Maria's thesis, and sometimes we all went out with him after class.

But back to the occasion in 1974, my two classmates were coming with me and were excited by the prospect of meeting the famous Manuel Puig for a drink. Merrily tipsy after a while, we all left the bar and wandered, chatting and laughing all the way back to my pad on King St., just south of Houston. Fortunately, roommate (and apartment renter) Merle was still at work. Somehow, the tipsiness landed us all naked in my bed, spontaneous participants in a symposium of flesh. Ana Maria and I, two nubile female bodies on the crowded creaking sofa bed, enjoyed discussing Maria de Zayas with each other but were not ready for this—and Manuel was clearly attracted to virile Gonzalo. As for Ana Maria, I thought she was straight as an arrow like that Spanish girl, a neighbor in Madrid, whom I had acquainted during my year in Spain, and whose parents frowned on our friendship because foreign girls and women had a loose reputation in Franco's Spain.

On a few occasions in the mid to late 1970s with another gay male friend—Jorge Oliva, a tall rugged Cuban poet who would die of AIDS in 1986—on beach weekends or smoking marijuana or sniffing coke, I did join threesomes or foursomes in those wild years. Casual orgies were not uncommon in those days among the bohemian or intellectual set in New York—I can't comment on nowadays. By the end of the 1970s, however, such adventures were pretty much past tense, a good thing considering the AIDS plague that was about to befall the gay world. Around that time and all through the late 1970s, when Emir and I had separated and I was living alone, I was thirty and at my most "experimental." Back to Merle's apartment in 1974, the final act of this forward foursome ended with Gonzalo doing Anna Maria, and Manuel amazingly doing me. Well, I thought, this certainly broke the ice.

Was sex, like *The Buenos Aires Affair*, yet another creation of his and mine, in which the title was identical in Spanish and English, the two of us a single duplicity, now collaborating in the biblical sense of the word? Or simply was it all a game Manuel and I played, maybe because we were both embarrassed to cross this barrier genuinely, in that room on King St. where the Sixth Avenue traffic was almost always on high volume. In that modest little room Manuel would arch one eyebrow imitating perverse Dirk Bogarde in Liliana Caviani's *The Night Porter*, feigning gestures that were fussily effeminate and yet sexually menacing. I feigned submission and did submit, like the young Charlotte Rampling playing a concentration camp victim, and I did feel what she acted, like a bedazzled waif in erotic anticipation.

Except of course, I didn't have her hungry green eyes, deep pools of lust, nor did I have her perfect long thin body, but I had my charms as we do when we are young. Manuel, contrary to his effeminate sense of self and modest definition of his private part as a "clitoris," was well endowed. He had all sorts of campy names for the penis and sometimes called it "berenjena" which is Spanish for eggplant which is, let's face it, a thick vegetable. As often is the case between Spanish with its fluidity and rhythms and English with its sharp angles, "berenjena" sounded more suggestive than eggplant.

Thanks to Sixties liberation, the Seventies were the real Sixties, the funky decade of wild sex for my generation, the decade of following one's affinities, of "seizing the moment," *carpe diem* and all that. Nietzsche was the reigning philosopher, giving us all license to act on impulses regardless of consequences. And there would be consequences. Manuel evidently felt freer to engage sexually with me because I was young, and, as he put it, not the motherly type of woman like other female friends. Carlos Fuentes had attached to me the dubious epithet "the Lolita of the Boom," no doubt based on the first time he saw me in Paris, dressed skimpily on a hot summer day, in the company of Emir. Before Carlos's eyes at that moment, Emir morphed into Nabokov's Humbert Humbert by the mere fact of his intimate alliance with a very young woman who, to boot, dared to translate gender-bending novellas by both Fuentes and Pepe Donoso about transvestites and homosexuality.

The spring of 1974, of my "Buenos Aires Affair" with Manuel in Manhattan, coming each week from New Haven, I would head down the Merritt Parkway to Riverside Drive. It was the sexy mid-Seventies and Barry White's deep sensual voice was on the car radio that delivered the "love machine" and other hot Motown sounds I anticipated with masturbatory images in my head, the imminent encounter. Sex or its fantasies can erase any troubling thought especially when we're young, and thus I would arrive at Norberto's apartment, my heart pounding, and ring the bell.

The apartment would be dark inside, the shades drawn, Manuel would have just showered and my first sensation, when he opened the door, was the clean smell of his freshly applied Pond's Cold Cream. This was the very same facial cream my mother and other women her generation used to wear, and for a while after our affair I would still associate the fragrance of my mother's generic skin cream with erotic ecstasy. Sex was the first order of business, before our editing session, as he preferred this sequence. Invariably we'd take our time, then leap out of bed, sheets and clothes strewn everywhere, get our clothes back on and from sexual athletes we turned into copy editors. So businesslike we focused on *The Buenos Aires Affair* on the page, the pleasures of the text, after playing the absurd roles of Leo and Gladys on Norberto's bed.

Ronald Christ who edited the Center's *Review* magazine in the 1970s, was a friend, or more precisely a "sister" to Manuel and observed that his (or her) romances with men never lasted long. Christ (pronounced like crisp with a "t") was not Ronald's real surname, but rather Turner; I can't remember the reason(s) for this, but it did raise eyebrows. Ronald also wrote that "Far less romantic though not dismissible was Manuel's occasional curiosity about a woman. So far as I know, these were boyish types, whom he described treating sexually like a boy." Once he said: "And she thinks she seduced me!" I couldn't help thinking Ronald was alluding to me though I wasn't boyish and, from what I could tell, Manuel didn't treat me like a boy and liked my female body just as he liked his men to be virile. The one time I tried using a dildo as the active partner, it was half-hearted. The boyish thing if that's what this was, was not my strong suit, though sex with women was beginning to seem a possibility. If Christ were alluding to me, maybe he astutely was predicting the fact that in 1978 I would begin, as mentioned, my first real same-sex relationship.

The last time Manuel and I had an intimate rendezvous was in 1978, after the publication of *Kiss of the Spider Woman* in New York and when Manuel finally had his own apartment on Carmine Street. He was happy to have a room of his own, for sure, so close to Christopher Street. We had sex here, I believe, a couple times, and even did cocaine once. His apartment was a tiny little studio with a view of the bustling street life, and we were not alone on this last occasion. We were a sort of threesome with one of his crushes, a Brazilian journalist, who looked so ordinary to me, and looked like he would have preferred to make love to me. Seeing them together I could understand that Manuel really did want, on some level, to be the wife of a typical "normal" man. Though curious to see this act in real life, I felt estranged and, as they say in French, *de trop*. In that scenario, one man entering another, I mainly felt despondent, I believe, that Manuel preferred to make love with a man.

Ultimately dalliances with Manuel led to a clash between the professional and the personal, shattering our bond of camaraderie; he was homosexual, after all, and the flip side of adoration was misogyny. Sometime later when we were reunited as friends again, we made up and joked that he had been my first lesbian affair, which in some way was true. What was also true about our dangerous liaison was that intimate relations without total trust—a common malaise we shared—are more about power than love. Manuel was Toto, the boy who struggled with his sexual identity in an oppressive society in *Betrayed by Rita Hayworth*, and who would learn to manipulate friends to secure what he wanted or needed. Manuel was transparent in his manipulativeness, like the little Toto, and this character flaw mostly amused his friends. It was, after all, a reasonable strategy for one who felt he was an underdog. As a graduate student, I was certainly not on top of the heap either.

More to the point, the adage "never mix business with pleasure" once again rang true. Our private conduct had made it easier for Manuel to ask me to translate *Kiss* for a flat fee of $2,000 that he would pay out of pocket without the guarantee of a publisher's contract or "letter of agreement" to protect my rights. This deal felt shaky and the whole incident became unpleasant for all concerned, plus I was about to take on my first formal position as professor, which, considering my minimal experience with teaching, required my full attention for the first year at least. He was miffed that I had convinced him to accept the previous contract for *The Buenos Aires Affair* which had stipulated a very small percentage of sub rights cut out of the author's share for me as translator: a big fuss over nada as the book was not a commercial success.

Unlike most writers, he had refused initially to have an agent. But he finally came to his senses and, when we were discussing the "deal" he was offering me, he had just acquired a top and very tough agent at ICM, the lantern-jawed Lynn Nesbitt, who had the withering interactive style of Anna Wintour; in my opinion she could stare down Adolf Hitler. I was invited to meet her in one of those modern office buildings on 57th Street: the meeting was brief. The intimidating Ms. Nesbitt was not about to let Manuel share his rights and royalties. Manuel and I had, therefore, our final blow up as I would not translate *Kiss of the Spider Woman* without a contract or letter of agreement with a publisher. The latter solution ensured that the publishers' commitment to the translator would be as minimal as possible. While I did stand firm on principle—nowadays, with the PEN contract, translators have undeniable rights—I would regret (after the feelings cooled down) not translating his most famous book.

We got over all this several months later, but by that time it was 1979 and he was moving to Brazil and so our paths diverged for the next ten years. When he moved to Mexico in 1989 and came to California early that year, we were very cheerfully, with our usual giggly rapport, reunited. I had invited him to give a talk at the university in Santa Barbara, and he accepted with affectionate enthusiasm to visit me. In those ten years (as I later wrote in my biography *Manuel Puig and the Spider Woman: His Life and Fictions* that came out in 2000), I was somewhat shocked and quite saddened by how dramatically Manuel had aged; he looked gray and tired, or maybe just stressed, his posture hunched over.

I picked him up on Melrose, in Los Angeles, at the house of producer David Wiseman and drove us up to Santa Barbara where he would give a talk I had arranged. He would spend a couple of days with me going over our final translation draft of *Tropical Night Falling* for which I finally received a bona fide contract. In the end this was a kind of poetic justice. Manuel told me he had concluded that I was his best translator and he wanted to make up for past misunderstandings. He was invited and received with gusto by UCSB where a large audience loved him, as usually happened when he spoke in public. His talks were disarming in their humility, mischievous in their modesty, in brief, the Puig charm.

On the ride up to Santa Barbara, I asked him which writer he felt was most influenced by him, and, without having to think hard, he said what I already sensed, not a novelist, but the very talented and today even more famous Spanish film-maker Pedro Almodóvar. Manuel was particularly struck by a wickedly subversive early film titled *What Have I Done to Deserve This?* Almodóvar had absorbed Manuel's camp mode, a particular mixture of sincerity and nutty humor, of profanity and absurdity, very Puigian indeed.

On that visit, he slept on the convertible sofa in the living room of my tiny, rented gardener's cottage, but he suggested half in jest, half seriously, that we "do it" again in nostalgic homage to our past peccadillos. I was forty-two, no longer that young girl: the years had passed, and my eroticism had veered in another direction. I was no longer interested, no longer attracted to Manuel as I had been back then. I felt sad about this clear sign of the passage of time, but also relieved that he didn't insist or take it to heart. I did love him and always will remember him with great fondness for an old friend with whom I had shared an unforgettable part of my life.

July 1990 was about a year after the last time I had seen him in Los Angeles at the opening night of his play, in glamorous circumstances very apropos of Manuel, surrounded by celebrities who adored him as much as he them, including the old-time hoofer Ann Miller, the very tall Daryl Hannah, Ann Bancroft and Mel Brooks. Manuel had invited me to the Mark Taper theater to celebrate the premiere of *The Mystery of the Rose Bouquet* starring Jane Alexander and Ann Bancroft. Here was yet another great success in his career, which, I believed, would flourish for years to come. Manuel was finally entering the mainstream. Speaking of which, it now seems obvious that Stephen King's title *Rita Hayworth, or the Shawshank Redemption*, a prison tale like *Kiss of the Spider Woman*, could have been a rejoinder to (my translation) *Betrayed by Rita Hayworth*. Anyway, we had great hopes for future collaborations.

But this was not meant to be. When the phone rang that July, I was just returning home from Big Sur on a romantic holiday; the good cheer was instantly replaced by panic and grief. It was Bruce Benderson with the heartbreaking news that Manuel had died in Cuernavaca after emergency gallbladder surgery. We couldn't believe it. It simply wasn't fair: he was so vital still, only in his mid-fifties, full of projects, looking forward to enjoying a new life in Cuernavaca in the most beautiful home he had ever owned. When the *New York Times* obituary came out the next day, Bruce in New York and I in Santa Barbara commented over the phone that Manuel at least had the last laugh, as the obit read that he was survived by his two daughters in Mexico.

When I saw those words in print, I couldn't help smiling through the tears. I knew that the hasty or literal-minded reporter hadn't realized that his gay informants, Manuel's two younger friends in Mexico City, were alluding to themselves as the "daughters" of Rita Hayworth, respectively Rebecca with Orson Welles and Yasmine with the Shah of Iran.

I have wondered how life would have been had I done *Kiss of the Spider Woman.* As it turned out, Manuel had a lot of trouble with the translation he had thought "anyone could do" (do with his help, that is). In this case the "anyone" was his agent and our mutual friend Tom Colchie who was a distinguished translator from the Portuguese. I suppose that, had I translated the bestseller, I might have won more prizes for translation or been invited to film festivals. Or maybe not. In any case, as Borges's closest friend Adolfo Bioy Casares, implied in so many of his stories, with stoic acceptance: "Character is destiny."

6

With Bioy in the Bois de Boulogne

Almost all of Adolfo Bioy Casares's "fantastic" stories and novels involve some adventure, usually a misadventure, as in his late novella *Adventure of a Photographer in La Plata.* "Aventura" in Spanish also means "affair." Speaking of cognates, the cognate word in Spanish "fantástica" is closer to its original meaning than the adjective "fantastic" in English. In Spanish it singularly denotes "fantasy" as in "imaginary" or "uncanny." When we say "fantastic" colloquially in English it is a hyperbole, usually meaning "great" or "fabulous" which, like fantastic, comes from a more specific noun, in this case the noun "fable."

Bioy Casares was certainly "fantastic" meaning "fabulous." Fabulous to read, the stories and books of Bioy Casares belonged to a "hybrid" genre, invented by Jorge Luis Borges, called "literature fantástica" in Spanish that also could be translated as "fantasy" literature. I first met Adolfo Bioy Casares and his wife Silvina Ocampo in July of 1971 in Buenos Aires, a city which at that time looked like an elegant London or Paris. It especially evoked New York as well as the capitals of Europe, but was perhaps even more stunning than any European city, because of its uncanny geographical location on the southern tip of the South American continent.

Emir, whom Bioy would one day describe affectionately to me as "muy gaucho," was, again, my emissary. "Muy gaucho" or "muy criollo" depicted Uruguayans because porteños like Bioy Casares and Borges opined that their neighbors, also called "orientales" because Uruguay was on the eastern bank of the River Plate, were simple or straightforward, provincial or roughly hewn compared to those city slickers, the sophisticated citizens of Buenos Aires. They felt this in a fraternal way, as if Uruguay were a younger brother or sister. Emir may have had a "gaucho" side, but he was certainly as cosmopolitan as Bioy, if not more so.

Generous with his friends, Emir invited me and our friend Alfred MacAdam (who was then Emir's junior colleague at Yale, on a fellowship in Brazil that summer) to join him on this visit to a writer who was already important to us "estudiosos" of Argentine literature in general and of Bioy Casares in particular. We regarded Silvina, then, as a minor though interesting writer, an attitude lamentably typical of how women writers were still cast in a marginal role in mid-century and beyond. Despite the dominance of the patriarchy, the time was more than ripe, however, to give the remarkable women poets and writers of Latin America their due.

At twenty-three it was exhilarating to walk along the elegant streets to the grand Buenos Aires apartment of two famous writers—known also for their wealth and their unconventional marriage. I see myself then a bit like that naïve American played by Owen Wilson in Woody Allen's *Midnight in Paris*, suddenly stepping into the Roaring Twenties or the *fin de siècle*. But now we were stepping out of a creaky wrought iron art-nouveau lift onto the penultimate floor of an elegant building on Posadas in the exclusive barrio of Recoleta.

Bioy Casares was sixteen or seventeen in 1930 when he first became intimate with his mother's friend Silvina Ocampo, a brilliant and seductive woman eleven years his senior. By marrying Silvina ten years later, Bioy formed an alliance with one of the wealthiest families in Argentina, the Ocampos. Silvina would be, like Borges but maybe more so, Bioy's kindred literary spirit until her death in 1993. The six Ocampo sisters shared this fine old edifice in fashionable Recoleta. Nearby was the historic cemetery where rich or important citizens were buried, including Evita Peron—though the real corpse was probably elsewhere. Each floor of the six-story Posadas building consisted of a single apartment, ample and labyrinthine, home to each of the sisters, complete with servant quarters.

The most prominent of the six Ocampo sisters was Victoria, the eldest, a woman of letters who in the 1930s began to preside over a world-class cultural salon in her home. From 1940 on, this was a stately mansion in eclectic French and Victorian style, originally the family's summer home called Villa Ocampo, in the ritzy suburb of San Isidro outside of Buenos Aires, which today is a UNESCO site and museum. The house is surrounded by an historical garden and hosts an important collection of art, furnishings and a library of 12,000 books, photographs, letters and the personal papers of Victoria Ocampo. Among the distinguished visitors (some of them reputed to be her lovers) invited by Victoria were the poet Rabindranath Tagore, Igor Stravinsky, Le Corbusier, Albert Camus, Graham Greene, Federico García Lorca, André Malraux, José Ortega y Gasset, Antoine de Saint-Exupéry and Saint-John Perse (Alexis Léger).

When we arrived at the building on Posadas, the doorman told us which floor, and waved us toward the antique elevator. When we finally arrived at Bioy and Silvina's apartment—it was a slow ascension—and knocked on the entrance door, it was opened, after a leisurely pause, by a maid in uniform. The trappings of wealth were like something from another age, I thought, at least from my very modest middle-class background in upper Manhattan, and part of me wished to have what I imagined to be the opulent life of these wealthy Euro-Argentines. The attractive young maid had a darkish complexion—was she from an indigenous "criollo" background or was it the dim light in the entrance? She led us from the shadowy foyer through another hallway into a grand book-lined salon with ceiling-high windows. Here was the motherlode: a vast personal library of dark wooden shelves rising from floor to lofty ceiling.

The young housekeeper invited us to sit on a sofa and told us to await "los señores" Bioy and Silvina; we were content to admire the majestic room and also curious to wander over to the books. A few years later in New York, Mauricio Muller, Emir's Jewish-Rumanian friend from Montevideo and a former journalist who looked like a character in a Lubitsch comedy, remarked that for him, Silvina was the most ingenious of the famed Bioy-Borges-Ocampo trio, the one whose wit and conversation he enjoyed most. Not only seductive, but more spontaneous or more approachable in her social behavior than her debonair husband and the pithy Borges. Cherchez la femme, or behind every great writer is a great woman and vice versa as in this case she too was an ingenious writer, but in a style very distinct from her confreres.

Bioy, called by his paternal surname rather than by his first name Adolfo (Adolfito was reserved for family and childhood friends), was the first, perhaps the more enthusiastic, to enter, with spry athletic steps, as if assuring his audience that he had been an excellent horseman and tennis player. He was a surprisingly slight and strikingly good-looking man in his mid-fifties with a V-shaped torso and dressed impeccably in a three-piece gray wool suit—July was winter in the southern cone. His hair was gray, headed for white, and he had thick bristling eyebrows, smiling blue eyes, and a strong sensual mouth: lithe and elegant, he had the air of a British aristocrat.

The saying goes that the Argentine speaks Spanish like an Italian, dines like a Frenchman, and dresses like an Englishman. This adage fit Bioy like a glove, except that his speech had a "criollo" lilt, native-born and refined, not like the Italianate slur of a more recent wave of immigrants. That local city slang, a mixture of Italian and Eastern European jargon called lunfardo, had been parodied with savage amusement by Bioy and Borges in the volumes of satirical detective tales they wrote in collaboration, penned by various pseudonyms borrowed from their respective ancestors, such as the famous Bustos Domecq.

I don't remember Silvina's entrance, perhaps because I was mesmerized by her spouse, but I do recall her already seated in an armchair, and that she was an arresting apparition wearing dark glasses and a stylish pantsuit. This petite, sharp-featured woman with jangling bracelets, the ice in the glass of whiskey she held in her hand also jangling, had a nasal voice—an imperious intonation, I learned, that was common amongst the "rancid" Argentine aristocracy. At one point, she was standing behind me and gently massaging my shoulders, exclaiming "how young you are!" I felt both flattered and embarrassed.

From that initial meeting I recall very little, unfortunately, except that Bioy, the infamous ladykiller, looked at me in a paternal yet flirtatious manner typical of an older man's response to a young woman he has just met. The conversation that ensued, mainly between Emir and the glamorously eccentric couple, was lively with good humor, anecdotes about common friends, the alarming errors and excesses of Latin American politics and allusions to local literati and to books they admired or criticized. Alfred and I sat rapt, not daring to jump in, as Emir and his two acquaintances resumed a dialogue that seemed as if it had been interrupted only moments earlier but had taken place years ago.

Emir and I were staying during those days in Buenos Aires, several blocks away from Posadas, at the apartment of Marta Fernandez, a feisty Argentine bookseller who lived in New York and who in those years owned a Latin American bookstore on the upper east side of New York. Marta had offered us her comfortable duplex filled with objects of art and enticing books, which faced the Recoleta Cemetery. (If you didn't know you were in Buenos Aires, you would confuse the Recoleta with the famous Père Lachaise in Paris.) The next day Bioy called Emir to invite both of us (not Alfred, about to rejoin his wife Barbara in Brazil where he was doing research) to dinner at their home with Silvina—and "Borges will join us." Emir was then finishing his biography of Borges commissioned by Dutton, which would be also the first biography to discuss Borges's personal life, and he was to meet with Borges on two or three occasions during our Argentine sojourn.

I had already met and spoken with Borges—a veritable guru to so many of us—a year or two earlier in the United States when Emir arranged for him to give a lecture at Yale. I doubted he would remember me from that brief occasion, but miraculously he did. At Yale I had dared to ask him about the influence of

Marcel Schwob's *Imaginary Lives* on my favorite Borges book then, *Historia universal de la infamia* (*A Universal History of Infamy*), a droll baroque exercise about felons or criminals about whom little is known, in which the author disguises fiction as biography or vice versa.

My question had to do with Schwob's series of brief fictional biographies, the last of which was based on scandalous hearsay about the heinous "body snatchers" Burke and Hare, who stole (and ultimately committed murder to provide) corpses for Dr. Knox because dissection for scientific purposes was forbidden in Victorian Scotland. The Wildean euphemistic style of this story, directly reminiscent of De Quincey's ironic essay "On the Fine Art of Murder," had significantly influenced the style of Borges's earliest stories.

During those twelve days in Buenos Aires in 1971, as Emir's consort, I was meeting the crème de la crème of Argentina's intellectual and artistic life: the witty, kinetic film-maker Torre Nilsson, a big fellow in thick glasses, and his vivacious wife, the writer Beatriz Guido; journalist Homero Alsina Thevenet—slight, fast-moving, quick-witted—who had an identical mustache and could imitate Groucho Marx even better than Guillermo Cabrera Infante; the clever bitchy nasal-toned José "Pepe" Bianco, novelist, short story writer and former editor of *Sur* magazine, and sexy, curly-haired Luisa Valenzuela and her self-possessed mother Luisa Mercedes Levinson, both of them novelists. We also spent time with the new, exciting novelist Manuel Puig, whose first novel, by the time I met Bioy, I already had translated. As mentioned previously, we were starting work on our next project together, the translation of his second book which would become *Heartbreak Tango*.

Dinner at the Bioys was, literally, a surreal event. Here I was, with Borges, Bioy and Silvina Ocampo who, along with Silvina's oldest and most famous sister, Victoria, founder of *Sur* magazine, had been the core of Buenos Aires's "Bloomsbury" group of the 1930s and 1940s. The trio whose company we were honored by that night had played the fringe role of subversives in Victoria's literary salon, constantly deflating high-minded conversations with biting humor. And here I was, seated as if I were a hyphen between two master dream-weavers, Borges and Bioy, and facing their muse Silvina.

When we had entered Bioy's and Silvina's house that evening, I was struck again by the low lighting as we were ushered in by the same attractive young maid, who again led us into the roomy salon, which this time seemed tidier than the previous afternoon of our initial visit. And, as if a theatrical effect were sought, Silvina was the first to enter, graciously offering us cocktails.

The pretty young maid silently served us courses of overcooked food which, I later learned, was typical of Silvina's kitchen; they were beefeaters like most Argentines, but they liked their steak well done. In that low lighting, between Bioy and Borges and under the gaze of Silvina, it felt like I was the unsuspecting young guest in a horror movie, in danger of being seduced by not so ageless vampires, with only Emir to defend me. The dinner conversation seemed to continue the dialogue begun that previous afternoon, this time more intense with Borges present: a lively duel of literary commentaries, remembrances and gossip filled with local fauna of which I caught references here and there. I believe we also mentioned my hopes of translating Bioy's novellas as well as Silvina's stories and both Bioy and Silvina responded enthusiastically as they knew that my first translations of Cabrera Infante and their friend Manuel Puig had been well received by critics. During dinner, aside from the excitement to be amongst these legendary figures, I kept hoping my Spanish didn't sound too gringa.

Almost a year later, with Emir's support I convinced my editor at E.P. Dutton to take on the first of several works of fiction by Bioy Casares which I would translate during the period from the 1970s to the mid-1990s. My correspondence with Bioy began that same year, 1971, with the excuse of sending him a story of his I translated.[9] There was an obvious mutual crush, but this was also an opportunity to request permission to translate his novella *Plan de evasion*. This novella, *A Plan for Escape*, published in 1945 with sinister German and French allusions to World War Two was a send-up of H.G. Wells's *The Island of Dr Moreau* that takes place on Devil's Island, the cruel French penal colony.

I wish I had titled it more colloquially as "Escape Plan" or "A Plan to Escape"— published initially by Dutton, then reissued by Graywolf Press. Some of the letters here are to be found in the "Suzanne Jill Levine archive" in the Lilly Library at the University of Indiana, Bloomington. I have tried to capture their tone in my translations. The Buenos Aires trip helped this translation; I had been trying to find the phrasing for the weird nasal voice of a minor character, a weird military orderly named De Brinon—Bioy borrowed this name, I later learned, a French politician who in France that had collaborated with the Vichy government. After meeting Silvina and Pepe Bianco, the strange nasal timbre of Silvina's voice, like that of their close friend Pepe Bianco, editor-in-chief of the literary magazine *Sur*, fit the description of De Brinon's voice. It was funny (in both ways) that these people whom he loved might be models for a sinister character, but then again, the only novella Bioy and Silvina wrote together (in 1946) is titled "Where There's Love, There's Hate."

Around the same time, for Knopf, Emir was editing with Thomas Colchie a two-volume anthology in English of Latin American literature; for this project Emir asked me to translate Bioy's story "The Myth of Orpheus and Eurydice," about a violent Peronist incident in 1953 in Buenos Aires. I sent this first translation to the author himself, hoping that he would feel well-served by my rendition. Mail from Argentina then (and probably still today) took weeks to arrive. When I finally received his letter it not only made my day, but it felt, in a coded way, like a love letter, and would be the first of many.

The letter came all the way to New Haven from "Rincon Viejo, Pardo," the Casares family ranch "Old Corner" in the town of Pardo (a word indicating a brownish color) where in the late 1930s he had written his famous novella *The Invention of Morel*; here (translated as faithfully as possible by me) is the relevant excerpt:

Rincon Viejo, Pardo, March 8, 1972

My Dear Jill:

Thanks for the letter and for the translation. About the latter: great suspense for the moment, to be expounded later.

I hadn't answered you until today, because for a time that has seemed immemorial, I have spent my season in Mar de Plata lying face up, dedicated to examining, in careful detail—which has struck me as sinister—the ceiling. It was nothing, lumbago; but, what a lumbago! That finally ended with a single injection, applied after fifty useless ones upon the advice of the father of my daughter's literature professor. There's nothing like literature.

The lumbago interrupted the progress of a short novel "Los desaparecidos de Villa Urquiza" that I had begun with great hopes. But there is always something to be gained, as a Mexican general once said, and if I suffered over not writing (incredible as this seems), I spent who knows how many hours a day thinking about the little novel. As I watched it grow ... the novel and I became more intimate. Now I understand that before the lumbago, like an irresponsible chap, I was going to write something about which I was completely ignorant.

Back, finally, to your translation. I wouldn't like to be unfair to others but I think, Jill, that it's the best that's been done with a text of mine. In general, the task of the translator consists of simplifying a text by weakening it, leaving us with an evident mystery: Why did someone write (of course for this question there is never any answer) and why did someone else take the trouble to translate? Any author who doesn't want to abandon right there and then his profession should abstain from such depressing readings. With "The Myth of Orpheus and Eurydice" the danger, for me, is pride. I assure you that I have caught myself in the mirror, reading your pages with a beatific smile (from ear to ear), which could only correspond to the phrase: "How well I write!" "The Myth of Orpheus and Eurydice" does not read like a translation but as an original written with confidence, with intelligence and with grace.

As if I believed that those merits were also my own, your translation stimulated me to confront the continuous difficulties that fetter me in the composition and writing of The Disappeared ....

This polite yet confidential letter from Bioy, who had had a tedious summer (from what I could surmise) lying around in pain was, even if exaggerated, immensely gratifying. The novel he was writing ("The Disappeared of Villa Urquiza") would be published a couple of years later as a tragi-comic love story with a science-fiction subplot under the title *Dormir al sol*, alluding to the danger of insolation for dogs when they fall asleep in the sun. A few years after I did *Plan for Escape*, I translated *Dormir…* for Persea Books, where it was published as *Asleep in the Sun* in 1978, later reissued by New York Review of Books Modern Classics Series. I translated five books by Bioy between 1972 and 1992.

Like Borges and other Argentine writers, Bioy translated English and Romance language foreign literary works for the literary journals they all supported. Close collaborators Bioy, Borges and Silvina, also translated short fiction for a landmark 1940 anthology of fantastic literature the three had edited in Argentina. He could fully grasp, on many levels as he does in this letter, how my translation stimulated his own writing. To begin with, considering his apparent image of himself as an invisible writer, the fact of being recognized via translation had been a stimulus. Bioy was a man who did not like to advertise himself and who usually expressed himself with a modest courtesy tinged with irony, a reserve typical of well-educated members of the Argentine upper classes. Others weren't so refined, of course.

Paul Valéry spoke of the "Esprit" as the producer of Literature. Borges greatly admired Valéry's acute observation and thus ran with it by placing literary creation in the hands of humanity, as the product of a communing chain of generations of writers and readers through the ages, rather than as the sacred words of solo consecrated authors. Eros and logos are inseparable in the act of creation, as they can be in the act of translation—and the misogyny of culture reveals itself in the infamous French saying that compares translations to women, or "les belles infideles." If beautiful, they must be unfaithful.

Again, before I met the man, I had already read (chuckling all the way through) *Plan de evasión*, the first novella of his I would translate. I was predisposed to adore the author of this comic yet tragic satire on fascism, mad scientists, man's shadowy existence and the blind fatality of love, and so when meeting this suave fine-looking man on that southern winter day, I was already a bundle of enthusiasm. Adolfo Bioy Casares, debonair and witty, was the Argentine Cary Grant, it could be said. Manuel Puig, adept at comparing real-life people to movie stars, insisted that, over the front desk at the *Sur* office, the full-length photo of Bioy as a young man always reminded him of the dashing young Burt Lancaster.

Writing can play with time in ways that life cannot. The last letter I received from Bioy would be over a quarter of a century later, in 1995, four years before he died at the age of eighty-five. *The Selected Stories of Adolfo Bioy Casares*, translated and edited by me and first published in English with New Directions in 1991, was the result of collaboration over several years, mostly by correspondence with Bioy but also with Emir, until late 1975. There's a scene at the very end of Puig's novel *Heartbreak Tango* in which the son of a lady who has recently died, follows her last wishes and sends the letters of her greatest (and unconsummated) love down the incinerator. As each letter is consumed by the fire, the reader glimpses bits and pieces, a passionate sentence, or a fragment, here and there, from the character of that young man who died long ago. Rereading these letters from Bioy, I recall (faintly now) the heartache of never seeing each other again and I also recall that translating them felt like a follow-up to my translations of those corny love letters in *Heartbreak Tango*.

Life is like translation, imitating fiction as it does in these letters from 1973.

January:

> Thinking of the color of your skin, of the light in your eyes, of the fragrance of your hair ....[10]

October:

> Darling Jill,

> Thank you for the good news from Dutton. But even more, thank you for being so charming and affectionate. Really, really, you are the best that has happened to me in a long time. I won't say "in my whole life" so that you don't

think I'm "exaggerating" but I am sure that if say in my whole life it's because it is how I am feeling now.

After our visit to the Chateau d'Amboise in June 1975, I received a letter the following fall in which he writes in amorous hyperbole:

September 1975:

My Love:

When I heard you play piano in Le Choiseul d'Amboise, I fell even more in love with you. I think that Suzanne Jill is the most beautiful girl (dressed and naked), the most intelligent, most refined, funniest, wittiest, who writes so well and is the most charming girl I have ever known

Except for ten days in 1973 and a month in 1975, Bioy and I were, as Marvin Gaye sang despondently, distant lovers. Our affair was little more than a dream, like many of his stories, a joyful dream during those moments when it was real. When we separated at the end of June 1975, with tears we promised to see each other again soon, somehow, which, of course never happened—until many years later when it was no longer relevant. A letter from Bioy in January 1982 certainly stresses the sadness of after: "What a nightmare this dream of life becomes: to

Figure 6.1 Adolfo Bioy Casares and Jill at his home in Cagnes-sur-Mer, France, 1975. (Photo credit: Hugo Santiago.)

find each other, enjoy each other, to separate for just a short time supposedly, and to miss each other for endless years."

Bioy's images here echo his stoic allusion in our conversation about infidelity in Paris in June 1975 when, on our eager way to an exquisite outdoor café in the Bois de Boulogne, circling Place Concorde in his elegant Citroen sedan with its floating suspension, he asserts somberly "one man's dream is another's nightmare." In the fall after that summer, Emir discovered my letters with Bioy Casares, and Bioy's dream was Emir's nightmare. Not a time I want to remember, as infidelities between intimate partners rarely have pleasant consequences. Fidelity and infidelity can be defined as two sides of the same act in translation, just as many wayward lovers argue: "aren't I being faithful to myself, to the truth?" Does literary translation, I wonder, open a connection with amorous behavior? Does fidelity or infidelity depend on the reader/lover's feeling/interpretation?

My translations of Bioy were "faithful" to his (and for that matter Borges's) Anglophile tenor, and to a form of writing that was *llana*, or plain, economic, restrained. Anglophilia was not out of step with aspects of the Argentine sensibility, mainly because many Argentines, like Borges and Bioy, had ancestors from the British Isles. Borges always claimed that Bioy led him from the exaggerated baroque to understated classicism but we can also say that, from the very beginning, this "classicism" was a shared "superstition" for them both. In a very early essay, "Two Ways of Translating," Borges summarizes the two "ways" as Classical vs Romantic, re-stating T.S. Eliot's "impersonality" of the poet (which emphasizes that the modern poet must move beyond the romantic cult of the individual) that differs from but still can be traced back to classicism.

My doctoral thesis (eventually an academic book published in Spain) grew out of my translation of *A Plan to Escape*. The dense allusions in the novella, led to my focus on the more than obvious conclusion that translation and literary criticism were parallel pursuits. "Intertextuality" was the theoretical buzzword of my graduate years—bringing into the foreground of literary studies the dialogue upon which texts are constructed—and this dissertation became an "intertextual" interpretation of Bioy Casares's two early novellas (the other being his more famous *Invention of Morel*) within the long tradition of utopia.

The translation led me to see these as exemplary narratives exposing the origins, evolution and procedures of Borgesian "fantastic literature." Borges's young disciple and collaborator Bioy Casares had been the first to define this invention as a "hybrid" genre encompassing narrative, poem and essay, detective story and science fiction, telling how fiction and literary criticism often merge.

Bioy's comedic yet nightmarish representation of the penal colony on Devil's Island not only evoked Kafka and the nightmare of the Second World War, but encapsulated a chain of texts and islands from Plato to the novels of H.G. Wells. Following Bioy's assertion in his introduction to the 1940 anthology of "la literatura fantástica" (edited by Borges, Silvina Ocampo and himself) that from the earliest myths to the mid-twentieth century, literature and fantasy were of one cloth, that most literature was "fantastic" and realism was a relatively recent artifice of the modern novel since the eighteenth century.

Literary criticism and translation were another pairing in my later critical articles and essays. When writing these essays, I felt that the writer whose text I was analyzing, like Bioy and other writerly conspirators, inspired, gave breath to translation mainly because he wanted, as Donald Keene put it, to make the "remote intelligible."[11] In these letters Bioy's ever-present politesse and modesty are always modulated by his irony.

September 5, 1972:

> As soon as I received your letter, I dashed one off—you're definitely going to laugh at my English—to Herder & Herder … I hope I didn't put my foot in my mouth when I said you'd be willing to translate for them. Shamefully I sent Herder & Herder French press cuttings on Plan …, because they're inflated and persuasive.

June 27, 1973:

> Did I tell you I finished the novel? Now I'm in the anguish of finding a title. Temporarily it was called "Rest Cure." Then I thought I found a splendid title: Refuge for a Long Night, but I discovered, or I was made to see by friends, that the adjective "long" placed a poetic emphasis of poor quality. For a few minutes I became enamored of Refuge for the Sad. All the gold turned into a windfall and the windfall, into nothing. The bad part is that the book is in print and if a miracle doesn't save me, it will be called Refuge… Who says that that miracle might not be Jill or Emir.

Bioy's courteous deference to Emir and myself, as the reader can surmise, had a persuasive charm. In a letter of November 22, 1974, Bioy mentions, "your doubtlessly excellent 'Sleeping in the Sun'" (his translation of the title *Dormir al sol*). I was never quite sure if this title worked. The goal was to produce a title that both sounded like an ordinary activity and yet could suggest hidden danger relevant to the novel's science-fiction plot. We decided to call it *Asleep in the Sun* for the practical reason of placing it at the beginning of publicity lists, but it could have been "Sleeping in the Sun." "Sleep in the Sun" would have been vague as Sleep could be a verb or a noun, but now that I think of it in these terms, more interesting. The title needed to signal the danger of being caught unawares, as when dogs fall asleep in the sun, in which what is seemingly harmless, or even soothing, is not.

The translation, informed by Bioy's presence, aimed to make the characters sound colloquial in American English. Translation theory might call this "domesticating" but for Bioy Casares this was simply good writing. Bioy's excellent ear for the spoken word extended to his capable sense of spoken English, which was uncanny considering how little time he had spent in the States (mainly New York and Washington, D.C.) though of course he had often been to England and, as a member of the *porteño* upper classes, lived in a bilingual Anglo-Argentine community.

The Argentine duo dubbed "Biorges" by Emir, as mentioned earlier, seemed like a third (fourth and even fifth) writer when they collaborated on satirical texts under various *noms de plume*. These publications helped spread the false impression that, for many years, Bioy was (outside of a small circle of friends) an invention not of Morel but of Borges. While "Borges" at times showed up as a fictional Borges, Bioy's existence seemed more tenuous, as if he were an impersonal cipher or quasi-anonymous in the literal sense of invisibility, certainly during his early life as a writer.

Borges's claim that Adolfito, his young friend, disciple and collaborator, led him to write in a more "classical" manner, away from the self-conscious baroque or *ultraista* pyrotechnics of his early experiments, also may have been only a generous gesture. By the time he had met the seventeen-year-old Bioy, Borges was an accomplished poet and essayist who was already rejecting *ultraísmo*, that is, the avant-garde fervor of his youthful years.

"Classical" as used here is almost a throw-away, in the spirit of Ezra Pound's "making the old new" to stress that it is not easy to pinpoint the subtleties of translating Bioy Casares. When he and Borges would camp up their heavy-handed parodies under pseudonyms such as Bustos Domecq, neither writer sounded like himself but rather like a third writer.

Bioy's economic style that imparted an ever-present irony with quirky understatement was not casual as it seems but a meticulous strategy that produced efficient stories, novellas, or even short novels. It is easier to define the "untranslatable" complexities of "baroque" texts where neologisms or notable knots of layered and ambiguous meanings are much more visible or tangible.

The smooth appearance of a transparent surface in Bioy's writing is deceptive. There is almost always an opacity in his "less is more" approach to language. His reader and certainly his translator must catch the hints or nuance or register of the words and phrases he uses. He had a keen ear for class difference in colloquial speech, and his narrators and characters invite the reader's laughter at unexpected moments, either because of wry depictions of clumsy behavior or because their utterances are buffoonish, pompous or corny. In brief, the challenge is to transmit his Kafkaesque humor, to reproduce his subtle mockery in foolishly banal words. One can feel Kafka's sense of the absurd in Bioy, and Kafka's familiar irony that the world almost always defeats the individual, in line with Bioy's vision. Like Kafka's exasperatingly banal dialogues, spoken language in Bioy Casares's stories becomes an empty rhetoric which veils a sinister or tragic reality. The cliché becomes emblematic of insidious alienation, and so it is crucial for the translator to mirror the nuances of such local commonplaces.

Such "commonplaces" pertain to realism, one might think, but the stories and novels of Bioy Casares, whether they begin on a realist note or are marked with a realist register, slip imperceptibly into what often feels like a dream. Another enthusiastic reader of Bioy pinpointed the role mistaken perceptions play in Bioy's versions of the fantastic, and we corresponded; his letter to me mentions the novel *The Dream of Heroes*:

> I agree with you about Bioy's humor, but what really strikes me is the fecundity and sheer hallucinogenic weirdness of his imagination. He seems to say that our daily life is not our real life, that the true meaning of our life lies somewhere else. In "The Dream of Heroes" this idea is reversed: Gauna [the hero] thinks the true meaning of his life lies in the events of the three nights of Carnival but in fact, if he only had the strength to resist fantasy, the real meaning of his life could be found in the ordinary that is Clara's precious love, which he unwisely loses.[12]

This perspective also rings true in a review by John Updike, in *The New Yorker*, speaking of Bioy's "need to confess the fact of artifice." Was the illusion of love itself, that is, our so-called "authentic" feelings for another, at the core of this "fact" of artifice?

Although Bioy seemed more man of the world than Borges where women and sex were concerned, I had the sense that at an early age, like Borges, he found reality a bit too real. His wealth and social status gave him certain privileges and perhaps limitations in his intimate life, just as, in Henry James's and Edith Wharton's vision, economic reality and (usually women's) emotional life were inextricably bound together. Helena Paz's "tell-all" memoir of Bioy's love affair with her mother Elena Garro (who at the time was married to Nobel-prize winner Octavio Paz) confirmed Bioy's comments to me about his childhood, as in the following incident he recounted, apparently, to Helena as a little girl aware of her mother's infidelity:

> "I was very jealous as a little boy; one day I fought with my mother, locked myself in the bathroom and with all my strength threw a wet soap against a wall and it slipped all over the bathroom." My mother never knew it—he told the story with contained rage, and I was surprised to see that the charming Bioy could have such attacks of jealousy.[13]

Incest, or Oedipus, lurks in the tales about Bioy's mother Marta Casares with whom a young Silvina Ocampo had been lovers before the latter became Bioy's wife. Bioy's childhood jealousy of that relationship adds a perverse element, almost as if his love or lust for Silvina were a revenge.

As a child, Bioy apparently disliked Silvina, but, at the age of sixteen, he was seduced by her in her car. A story of his I translated, "All Men Are Equal," alludes to this seduction, except that the boy's enthusiasm is displaced onto the car, which comically annoys the woman no end.

Bioy and Silvina would remain married to the end of their lives—she died in 1993, he in 1999. Both of them, but especially Bioy, carried on numerous affairs throughout the marriage. A vacillation between rebellion (toward his mother) and at the same time dutiful obedience to the requirements of his family and the society that sustained it seems a possible explanation, or perhaps more simply, money married more money. As he told Helena Garro once, "In those days, marrying an Ocampo was the supreme triumph in Buenos Aires."[14]

Bioy's ultimate wisdom perhaps was that the individual's fate was sealed from the start, overdetermined by character but also by one's socio-economic background, and I can extrapolate and have implied to an extent, my own story from this "stoic" perspective. In any case, Bioy could afford to accept an affinity with the Stoic philosophers of the ancient world, and so he believed and accepted that character is destiny, something we all (and I include myself) have to make peace with if at all possible. Writing (like sex) was a way to escape consciousness for Bioy, to immerse himself in the alternative world of fiction, a fantasy world, where he perhaps needed to evade the disturbing reality of Silvina's apparent affair with his mother. More than an established fact, this is popular hearsay disseminated by Helena Paz's memoir. Did Bioy negate or erase this scandal by marrying Silvina Ocampo? We will never know for sure, and best not to play shrink.

Reality can be a trap (or too real for comfort) and there was no way, in *The Dream of Heroes*, that the ordinary though precious love of Clara could have rescued Bioy's avatar Gauna. Bioy would spend his whole life, as one can see in hindsight, pursuing his phantom of liberty as a writer and a lover of countless girls and women. A member of the upper classes, Bioy had the luxury of countering the tenuous nature of reality by cultivating invisibility. Among the elite circles of River Plate culture, self-promoters like professional writers were seen as crass merchants. This value judgment unfortunately helped to seal his fate as a lesser-known writer, the inhabitant of an unreal, or more precisely, unrecognized world. It's worth noting that, in his late seventies, after he was awarded the prestigious Cervantes prize in 1991, Bioy Casares expressed second thoughts about upper-class snobbery toward the professional writer. He must have realized that he had arrived late to the party, passive or hesitant like so many of his protagonists.

Coda

The last occasion when I saw Silvina was in the summer of 1973 when Bioy and I had our first meeting in private. Well-located on Rue de Verneuil near Saint-Germain-des-Prés, David Bigelman's bohemian studio was the scene of my first tryst with Adolfo Bioy Casares. I don't think I really knew at that moment whether I was in love with Bioy's looks or his charm or his fame, or simply romantic love itself, the latter a creation of the brain which the heart then follows. Absurdly or not, I definitely was infatuated. The 5th, 6th and even the 7th arrondissements, in any case, were not this Argentine aristocrat's Paris, which was, on the contrary, the right bank, and especially the elegant 8th or 16th arrondissements where the wealthy dwell with spectacular views of the Eiffel Tower.

Silvina and Bioy invited me to a family luncheon around a big oval table in an ample and luxurious apartment in Paris, with a glorious view of the Eiffel Tower. Typical of wealthy Argentines, especially in the early part of the century, Bioy, Silvina and family were enjoying a leisurely sojourn in France. Their daughter Marta was Bioy's illegitimate daughter, whom Silvina had adopted with him. At the table Marta, who looked like a female version of Bioy, was accompanied by her first baby and her husband. The baby Victoria (named after her grand-aunt)

I would see again in Madrid in 1991, as a poised young lady, tall and well-dressed, accompanying her grandfather Bioy, by then a frail old man with an unsteady voice who was about to receive the prestigious Cervantes prize. I remember feeling slightly uncomfortable, an outsider, mostly about my own and/or Bioy's double life, in the atmosphere of that gathering of apparently spoiled rich kids and their distinguished elders.

Two years after this lunch I would be with Bioy in the Grand Hotel in Cannes, and Silvina would be calling Bioy one of those nights on the phone in our hotel room, complaining how much she was missing him in Buenos Aires. As Bioy said, one person's dream is another's nightmare. I co-translated (with Jessica Powell) Silvina Ocampo's posthumous novella *The Promise* for City Lights Press, thus titled because of an apparent promise Silvina had made to herself in her last years of lucidity. The promise was to write a novel but it is really a loose structure, a series of linked anecdotes filled with eccentric characters and surreal events. The main character is Silvina herself as the narrator literally afloat in the sea, slipping in and out of consciousness. These hallucinations touch on her unconventional marriage with Bioy, where love was perhaps only a fiction that dreamed of being real one day, just as Bioy is now a distant dream to me.

Toward the end of his life—Bioy died in 1999—we saw each other briefly in Madrid in 1991, as I mentioned, and then during a visit I made to Buenos Aires in 1992 to consult him on an edition of his works I was preparing for New Directions. But even though we corresponded from the 1970s through the early 1990s, the actual time together was, again, no more than a summer month (when I could escape to France) between 1973 and 1975, half a century ago. I am glad I got to help Silvina's "promise" into print, as faithfully (or unfaithfully) as possible, as I know she would have appreciated this gesture of friendship. *The Promise* is an intelligent and provocative book worthy of passionate readers.

Intermezzo

Here I am, now, over fifty years later, on the Central California coast, living in desirable Santa Barbara by the wild Pacific, trying to recover glimpses of my interlude with Bioy Casares in France in 1975, an ephemeral love story in the light of the Mediterranean.

How the beach and the sea always meant romance in the popular imagination, certainly in mine, stimulated by movies I saw as a kid in the 1950s such as *Where the Boys Are* or the melodramatic *A Summer Place* about forbidden love between American teenagers starring the teen idols then, I mean Troy Donahue and Sandra Dee. Then came my first teenage awkward attempts at romance, making out on the beach at night, during the summers, first in Rockaway and then on Fire Island.

*

But the sea in this story is not Fire Island's rugged Atlantic with silky sand beaches, beautiful dunes, and rough gray waters. It is June 1975 and I am with Adolfo Bioy Casares on a private tranquil Riviera beach, near Antibes, in gorgeous Juan-les-Pins with its blooming pink and crimson bougainvillea, gazing at the calm blue green water, reclining on a lounge chair. Blue and white parasols and comfy striped mats on wooden white chaise-longues, and beside me, the slim, blue-eyed, craggy-faced man (I always went for those Marlboro looks) who was a celebrated Argentine writer. A fleeting moment in the scheme of things that belongs to eternity or to this dream of life, figures in the sand fading in the bright sun, Juan-les-Pins, John-the-Pines, watching the ripples on a shining sea, ceaseless, blue now green.

That morning, we had an argument, over something trivial. Spats between lovers are a foolish waste of precious time. We hadn't spoken to each other yet when we arrived at the beach. We just lay there, each on a separate blue and white striped cushion. After a while I touched his hand—in the sun we both felt better—and he closed his hand around mine. He had beautiful well-proportioned hands. I leaned over and kissed him on the mouth, ran my fingers down his thigh, and relaxed back on the cushion. "You have such little hands," he said, "*tan pícara*, so naughty, your little hands."

After a while he said (in Spanish), "Let's have lunch." We got up but didn't go directly to a restaurant. I walked ahead of him, felt his eyes on my body as we moved along the wooden plank of that Riviera beach club. We reached locker no. 414. He tried to open it, couldn't. "I'm the only handy one around here," I joked, because I am not handy, and so I fiddled with the hole where the knob was supposed to be, and he finally opened it, despite what also were clumsy efforts. I stepped into the cabinet, sat on the wooden bench against the back wall. He closed the door, stood facing me, pressed my head gently against his body…

We dressed in our light summer garments. As we walked out, the smell of frying olive oil almost covered up the sea breeze. We climbed the stairs, walked across the park, got into the Citroen sedan with its sexy leather seats. We drove along the seaside route, and I touched his thigh, kissed his neck, laid my head on his lap, feeling as if our bodies had always belonged together. Had I felt this way about any other man or boy? I surely had for Emir, but now only Bioy existed.

We reached a restaurant facing the blue sea beyond a low wall, over a rocky part of the coast. It was called La Belle Tortue. The Beautiful Tortoise. Lunch started with melon and prosciutto—it wasn't as good as Vieille Antibes—and the waiters weren't as cute, either. He liked my flirting. We ate the usual—faux filets, haricots verts, cheese, fruit, the wine was a delicate crisp white, and we were both beautiful or so it felt to me at that moment. We drove home to that efficiency building of condos which had depressed me at first, after our long drive down from Paris, but I didn't care anymore. Once in the elevator I threw my arms around him and we laughed and hugged and kissed, and in the mirror, I saw my tanned young self with long auburn brown hair in a white and pink striped cotton top and those goofy pink bell bottom pants in fashion back then, loving him as I gazed at him too in the large elevator mirror. Wishing now that I could have held that image forever.

Making love is a French euphemism.

"There was also a great personal favorite, andouillettes served with an outstanding sorrel sauce. The wine…" When I ordered andouillettes upon our return to Paris—and the dish arrived at the charming corner restaurant in the 8th arrondissement—I was horrified. Two thick sausages smelled awful and looked like turds—He laughed, and ordered for me steak frites, his go-to Argentine favorite.

I would miss him for many years, without ever seeing him again until I did see him again when he was very old. Perhaps, I too had lived for a long time in his memory as his letters told me. But at the same time, why was I drawn to older men like Bioy and Emir? Wasn't I wasting the precious years of my youth with an impractical obsession, living with ghosts when I should have been with young men and diving full-heartedly into my youth and the present which, as we know, is all we possess? Or possessed, as (I think) Proust wrote, "not by the present but by a ghostly presence that distracts one from inhabiting the real, the present, the only thing that could banish suffering. Reality then becomes an absence, one that revives the flames of suffering by keeping illusory love alive."[15] As Manuel said to me on one of the last times I visited him on Carmine Street, "Because they are so much older, years from now you will be surrounded by ghosts, because those you loved will be gone."

Figure 6.2 Jill, New York, 1984 (photo credit: Nestor Almendros).

Part Two

Stops Along the Way

Entr'acte

The gray waves come galloping white like angry lions. They come tumbling like stampeding horses. Gray blue into white foam falling, filling the coves, sand banks flooded, sandy stretches of wooden houses, decks with chaise-longues along the blinding beach.

I sit on driftwood, look out to sea.

A whiff of honeysuckle along the paths of Fire Island. Tall shiny strands of grass, short pine trees—mosquito havens after rain.

*

Thoughts I wrote down while crossing the great bay on the Fair Harbor ferry back to the south shore of Long Island.

It is June 1981. Except for moments like this, feeling the breeze caress my face, smelling the fresh salt air, looking down at the rushing water, life sometimes seems like acting rather than being. Or seducing and being seduced, only to discover, one day, that maybe the only way to know love is to know that one is loved. Which person—I, one, she—is speaking? Like all pronouns "I" belongs to everyone and to no one. I have lived between two worlds, from my early twenties until now, between two ways of speaking: English, my first language, and Spanish, the language she translates. Which speaker is the real me? Neither, or both. From time to time, I have felt like Alice confronted by the stoned caterpillar seated upon the giant mushroom, who defies her imperiously to tell him who she really is.

7

Sketches of Susan

Manuel Puig first set eyes on the young Susan Sontag in the late 1950s in Paris. She was sitting at a table in the Café de Flore with another young woman. From comments he made to a friend, apparently, he didn't find either woman appealing. I imagine this meant because they looked too masculine from his cinematic point of view. Manuel's opinions often surprised me, and this was a case in point: Susan, as many have celebrated her, was extraordinary looking, especially as a younger woman, but I understood that she was not his type. As Manuel once said, for him Hollywood and the legendary actresses who were great beauties like Greta Garbo, Hedy Lamarr, Lana Turner, and Vivien Leigh were the ideals. All that ended in 1950 with Gloria Swanson's farewell in *Sunset Boulevard.*

When I first saw Susan Sontag in the 1970s, she was lounging against a window with her long legs crossed and resting casually on the windowsill. She was wearing her classic black turtleneck and jeans, and of course had her thick black hair with the famous white raccoon streak. I felt intimidated or hesitant to approach because I knew she had recently survived a bout with breast cancer, and I was concerned about how to approach her in a casual way without coming off as frivolous. Not only was she very serious in general, but she was battling with a serious disease. I have always smiled a lot—unlike your usual stone-faced academic or writer whose demeanor is meant to signify gravitas—and such apparent levity has sometimes been misread in sober circles. Finally, I took the initiative and went over to her when she was standing near the table covered with an ample spread of bagels, lox, cheeses and salads.

This was a brunch party in *Fiction* magazine editor Mark Mirsky's East Village pad where he and his Norwegian artist wife Inger were then celebrating their recent marriage. It was one of those walk-up apartments, at least three steep flights, where the bathtub was in the kitchen. The mood was festive and most of us were sipping champagne. I introduced myself, postponing my desire to prepare a bagel with lox, cream cheese and flourishes. She seemed to know who

I was or at least that I had translated Manuel Puig, because the first thing she said to me was a question: "Is Puig queer?"

She was not one for polite chitchat but this abrupt probe caught me off-guard. I think I only managed to reply blandly "of course" with my usual non-referential friendly smile, trying to show I was unflappable, but she had the air of expecting a more elaborate comeback from a supposedly clever translator of edgy avant-garde writers. Her question stopped me in my tracks because I wanted but didn't dare to follow her question with several of my own. The first would have been, well, after all, wasn't she "queer"? And then, how could she possibly not know that he was homosexual? And why did she use, instead of gay, the term "queer" which at that time was still pejorative? Or, and this made the most sense: was she inquiring, in code, if I were queer? Or maybe, also in code, was she trying to find out if I had slept with Manuel Puig? I didn't take the bait.

Starting in the 1980s the term "queer" became a radical category, signifying not only an esthetic but a broader range of human sexuality and a mainstay of cultural politics, but at the time I met Susan, "queer" still fell upon the ear as an insult, though more polite than "fag." I would like to think, now, that I had witnessed first-hand the trendsetter Susan Sontag in action, reinventing "queer" as cool, defiantly positive, radical, outside of facile definitions of sexual orientation and social identity—and the world would soon follow her lead.

In December 2004, the cancer Susan had been heroically battling for decades, finally, sadly, won the war, and she died having just turned seventy-one. Almost three years later, in 2007, her life's work was ungenerously disparaged in a feature article published in the *New York Review of Books*, the same journal she had been featured in for decades. I didn't doubt that the male author of the piece, a former friend of mine, was acting out, envious of her position as a "celebrity literary critic." It was important, I felt, for the reader to share my inside knowledge about him, and so I wrote (and published in the *NYRB* "Letters" section) an irate repartee to vindicate her. I took him to task because his goal evidently was to belittle a remarkable woman, and because I, like other women in the arts and in academe, was hyper-sensitive regarding attacks with such a patriarchal tone.

Of course, Susan had imperfections, including how she took herself so seriously or her lack of a sense of humor, especially as a novelist and film-maker, and she seemed even naïve at times in her unchecked enthusiasm for artists and causes. Still, there was no doubt that her boundless energy to engage every corner of culture was admirable: she was gutsy, brilliant, ethical and often hit the bullseye regarding her views on esthetics. She was a woman who defied the oppression of women by not making feminism her agenda. Or, simply, Susan didn't want her writing to be pigeon-holed by her gender. Women should be able to write about anything and in any way they saw fit.

*

I left New York in the 1980s for the West Coast, and after that East Village brunch, I didn't have any further encounters with Susan again until 1991, after she had written to me a letter about how much she liked my book on translation, *The Subversive Scribe*, which she described as "A continually lively and very generous book, full of lore and such a vivid and just account of how complex a process good writing is." This time we spent an evening together in Santa Barbara where I was teaching at University of California, Santa Barbara. It was April 18th: I know this from my journal, where I wrote "A magical evening." At that moment her arrival in Santa Barbara was a life saver sent from New York, a spirit picker-upper (which often was not the case with her) as I felt profoundly isolated, surrounded by a foreign state of mind called California.

She had come to the university invited by the Humanities Center to give a talk on one of her favorite writers and probably Latin American's most important nineteenth-century novelist, the Brazilian Machado de Assis. As her lecture fee was probably large, the host was a bit peeved, not because it wasn't an interesting presentation of, arguably, the most important Latin American novelist of the nineteenth century, but because her text had already been published in *The New Yorker*. It was unseemly, at least in those days, to give an invited lecture that was already published material. After her talk, I offered to take her out to dinner and for a tour of Santa Barbara. The professors who were her hosts seemed relieved (and somewhat intimidated), so I assumed that I was doing them a favor.

As we were driving around town a bit before landing at a restaurant, she remarked on a detail I had barely noticed—or had passed over as insignificant. The detail was the ornamental script on the street signs, and she asked if the street names were written with Chinese handwriting, meaning that they had been made by Chinese laborers who had been hired on the cheap to lay down the railroad tracks in California in the nineteenth or early twentieth century. I thought this rather interesting but didn't know the answer. When I did get to ask a Santa Barbara connoisseur if this were true, I was told that Susan's conjecture was whimsical. Apparently my first impression of the curlicue lettering—that it was simply a Santa Barbara touch—was closer to the truth, but I liked Susan's theory, all the same.

At dinner that night I spoke to her about wanting to do "real" as opposed to academic writing, as I had begun to attempt with *The Subversive Scribe*. "You must write. Shoot for the stars," she said. Without transition she added: "You look great. You must be doing something right." She told me of her affairs, and we shared stories of "our Cuban lovers." Her first longtime woman lover had been Irene Maria Fornés, the playwright whom I had once met when attending a play by her in New York with Lydia.

At one point, Susan mentioned Joseph Brodsky as a significant passion in her life, almost as a trophy affair, and she exclaimed how lucky I had been to have been so close to Manuel Puig. "Write about your affairs with them," she said. "Men are awful, they're cold," she said emphatically, "but women are devastating." At the time of her visit, Annie Liebowitz was her new partner, and she remarked with certain emphasis, "When it's over with your first lover, the second affair is sad, because you didn't have it when you needed it, so the second time is always too late." What she said toward the end of our evening touched me the most: she wrote essays when she was afraid to fail with her writing.

*

In fall 2003 I was on sabbatical in New York, and, because of a tempting job offer, almost decided to move back there. I remember lunch at Susan's preferred Japanese place down some steps and kitty corner to the St. Marks' bookstore on 3rd Avenue and 9th Street. She was eating some live sea urchin still throbbing on the plate, and I had ordered my usual cucumber roll, miso soup and a seaweed salad. She promptly remarked, "You're not having sushi?" as if to ask, "Are you a philistine?" I felt obliged to reply that I wasn't a big fan of raw fish, but what was worse was the shame I felt for being a wimp. I tried to squirm out of the impasse by mentioning the advice of a doctor, my brother-in-law, who never ate raw fish because of the bacteria and mercury. Susan poo-pooed this caution.

Nonetheless I guess it was hard to say no if Susan invited me to hang out, like the time she asked me to join her at BAM (Brooklyn Academy of Music): who could decline such an invitation? And so, I picked her up at her Chelsea penthouse, we went down to Chinatown (I am sure she ordered something too spicy for me) for dinner, and then we traveled to Brooklyn, to my relief, in a taxi. This lavish gesture delighted me, especially as I had been dreading the tedious subway ride. As a native New Yorker, I had been riding subways since age five, so they lacked the romance they had for my non-native New York friends. The subway ride was the main reason though not the only one I never went to

Brooklyn. I also had the foolish prejudice that only Manhattan was the real New York.

To me, the heavy gray German, Russian or Serbian magnum opus, whose title I don't remember, was hard (aside from the seat) to sit through, but, as to be expected, Susan was intensely focused on the play from beginning to end. I tried to hide my disappointment (so uncouth after all) knowing that she was enthralled and, besides, she knew all about the creator of the work and was friends with one of the actors. Friends in the audience approached her during the intermission to talk about it or simply to greet her; what a relief that they gathered around her. On that occasion, I felt caught in deep waters.

Perhaps the closest I felt to her was when she insisted upon introducing me, as I was staying in the West Village, to her affable hairdresser Rick who had worked in the world of high fashion. We met at his retro comfy salon, "Sip and Snip," on Waverly near 10th and sat in those swivel chairs facing the mirror like two women friends sharing a chummy moment, chatting about this and that, sipping tea with Rick as he snipped, darkened and washed Susan's graying hair. I liked that Susan didn't mind being seen in disarray as it were, with wet hair and covered by an unattractive smock; I liked that we were sharing a casual moment.

For the next few years, after Susan was gone, I would go to Rick's to have my hair done every time I was in New York. As he skillfully worked his magic, Rick enjoyed remembering her clever remarks or the stories she'd tell. Her most emphatic advice, I told him, were her parting words as we hugged goodbye after that first visit to Rick's. "Come back to New York, Jill, don't stay in California. Let the city roll over you." I thought about it a lot that year, but didn't follow her advice. New York is a tough city.

As an outsider from the west coast, Susan had the self-assured spirit and the mental power to make New York her own. New York is a part of me from birth and I believe it has been better for my own creativity to elude the steamroller I already knew too well—but I may be wrong. I watched her, the quintessential woman warrior a little worse for wear, head west on 11th Street to her next appointment, before the light turned green and I crossed the avenue.

8

Three Feasts with Neruda

In July 1991, at a conference in Santiago, Chile, where the winter climate was sunny and crisp, I was staying at the family home of Cecilia Vicuña, the Chilean poet and installation artist who lives in Tribeca. With Cecilia I met her delightful local friends, mainly a lively group of young poets, one of whom drove a few of us west to visit Pablo Neruda's seaside home, Isla Negra (Black Island), which had that name, I believe, because of the dark color of the sand. Emir and a New York friend of ours, the Argentine journalist Rita Guibert, had regaled me with their visit to the maestro at this rambling wooden beach house, a shack really, perched above a wild Pacific. Neruda's beachside sanctuary was generously decked with oversized toys and careful collections of beetles, the parts of old ships, and other items, some of them curiosities but mostly everyday things like bottle caps which took on a magical dimension in the domestic aura of the bard. Rita had interviewed Neruda and Emir had helped put together her book of interviews of the most famous Latin American writers, titled *Seven Voices*, which had brought her to Isla Negra.

The house had recently been established as a national museum. Before getting to the museum, we stopped at a simple traditional restaurant down by the beach, where we were served a feast from the sea and subtly delicious chilled white Chilean wine. During that day I had told the poets about my three meetings with Neruda, and we also spoke about a conversation I had had with Cecilia and Gonzalo Rojas, a lovely man and an excellent poet of the generation after Neruda, in which we wondered why Chile was so well endowed with poets. Both Cecilia and Gonzalo felt strongly that the spoken Spanish of Chile lent itself to the language of poetry partly because of its special music, fed by the resonance of ancient indigenous languages.

The first time I met Pablo Neruda was not in Chile but in Caracas, Venezuela, the spring of 1970. Emir already knew Pablo and met with him a few times in the 1960s when Emir was writing *El viajero inmovil*, a fascinating biography of the bard, yet to be translated and which should be titled "The Stationary Traveler."

Emir was very much the mobile traveler as a Yale professor and eminent man of Latin American letters; on this occasion, I was accompanying him to an international conference of Hispanic literature.

Emir and I at that moment were still a new couple, raising a few eyebrows even in that sophisticated environment. The literary high point of that visit was the invitation to an elaborate midday (starting around 3:00 p.m.) banquet in honor of the great Pablo Neruda, at the impressive contemporary many-leveled mansion of the novelist Miguel Otero Silva who, as mentioned earlier, was a well-heeled member of the Communist party. I was probably the youngest person at that august long table of about twenty distinguished guests—probably poets, artists, writers as well as wealthy patrons—including Pablo, a bear of a man with big light eyes, his attractive wife Matilde who had a down-to-earth simplicity, the bighearted host Miguel Otero and, of course, Emir. As it was over fifty years ago, I honestly cannot remember anyone else, even the lady of the house, but I was absolutely thrilled when they generously placed me next to the great bard himself.

It was the first time I ever attended a formal banquet—and as is customary on these occasions, a waiter or servant in a uniform brought a lavishly adorned silver tray from which each guest had to serve himself, and to boot I was left-handed. From the (for me) awkward angle I was served at, removing a modest portion of exquisitely prepared fish from the tray was tantamount to a juggling act. We're talking about an enormous tray with the whole fish, eye and all, and somehow reaching and transporting an appropriate portion to my plate turned into an undertaking fraught with elbows—a bit like slapstick. I've never been terribly handy; fortunately, the waiter was and he managed to balance the tray and deposit a serving in my plate with his other hand.

In any case, the *almuerzo* was exquisite, as Neruda was not only a committed communist but a well-known gourmet, or perhaps gourmand. The challenge par excellence was dessert: a whole mango accompanied by a little silver paring knife. The pleasant voice of Pablo came to my rescue when he saw my pained hesitation: "Jill" he pronounced correctly with the soft "g," "yo te lo corto," and he both gently and methodically cut my mango into edible pieces. To me this act of chivalry seemed like the attentions of a lover; I felt both honored and speechless, and blushing deep red, managed to thank him. Matilde announced as the coffee was brought in that Pablo was going to take a siesta and so the great man beside me got up and—as if by magic—vanished into the vast labyrinth of that luxurious home.

The second meeting came a year or two later in New York, after a rousing public reading by Neruda at the 92nd Street Y. Everyone who was anyone in the world of poetry was there, including Allen Ginsburg, and Yevgeny Yevtushenko wearing a pink shirt, critics and journalists from every major newspaper or magazine. Afterwards a select group which included Emir, myself and Neruda's English translators, were invited to the Central Park West penthouse apartment of Chilean art historian Leopoldo Castedo (art professor at SUNY) and his lively petite spouse, Carmen Orrego, also a poet, who was generously orchestrating tapas as well as drinks for everyone. All of us sat around the great Pablo: Castedo, Emir, the poet translators including the blustery Robert Bly and suave Nathaniel Tarn with his adopted British accent. We were transfixed, listening to the great man tell a story about a fabulous sea beast that had washed up on the shores of Isla Negra right in front of his house—the museum I would visit twenty years later.

The third and final event was by far, for me, the most momentous: in February or March of 1972, at the Chilean embassy in Paris where Emir and I were the sole guests. Recently appointed Allende's ambassador to France, Pablo and his wife Matilde co-hosted, in their private ambassadorial quarters, our intimate dîner à quatre, a simple dinner prepared exquisitely à la française, starting with an aperitif in their living room. Here I could actually hug one of the toys, a giant stuffed lion almost the size of the poet himself. The pièce de résistance of this delicious French repast for the poet was the aperitif, his own invention, he proudly noted, a cocktail served in long elegant champagne flutes, a kind of kir royale with the juice from a berry that grew, he declared, only in the Arctic Circle.

Over a year later we would hear, amidst all the disturbing news from Chile, of Neruda's sudden death. We knew that he was battling cancer, though no mention was made during our dinner, nor were there any tell-tale signs. Still, we all suspected that his death, during the coup that destroyed Allende, was not due to his advancing disease but rather an undercover assassination. Pinochet needed to rid Chile of its Marxist heroes; the dark era of the military dictatorship loomed, and Chile would not rid itself of Pinochet until 1990.

9

Carlos Fuentes on Central Park West

The sudden death of Carlos Fuentes in 2012 in Mexico City felt like the end of an era, like the passing of the iconic Gregory Peck who had played the *Old Gringo* in one of his last films. Based on Fuentes's novel about the final days of the satirical American journalist Ambrose Bierce, who died mysteriously in Chihuahua during the Mexican Revolution, the movie would have foundered had it not been for the captivating portrayal of Bierce by Peck, who was appealing and charismatic despite his stiff acting style. According to historical accounts, the gringo journalist had a strong bond with Mexico. Fiction is inevitably autobiography too and, in some ways, Bierce was a mirror image of the cosmopolitan Carlos Fuentes, who moved with ease between two worlds as a Mexican with deep connections to the Anglo world—and in 1975 would become Mexico's ambassador to France.

Carlos's close friend, the Chilean Pepe Donoso, a less conspicuous member of the brotherhood that consisted of Carlos Fuentes, Julio Cortázar, Gabriel García Márquez and Mario Vargas Llosa, wrote an engaging "personal history of the Boom," where he stresses, "Looking, as always, at the phenomenon from my personal point of view, I see the Mexican Carlos as the first active and conscious agent of the internationalization of the Spanish American novel of the 1960s."[16]

Fuentes was a pivotal figure as the first Boom novelist but also because he generously supported his fellow writers, like Gabriel García Márquez who was still unknown in the early 1960s. At one point, Gabo, as the Colombian was nicknamed, was practically starving in an attic in Paris until Carlos Fuentes came to the rescue. In Mexico, Fuentes hosted Gabo and his family, enabling the Colombian to finish his most famous novel. Fuentes's generosity of spirit was "an expression of the grass roots of politics in the world of literature; he understood that writers need defenders, they need champions."[17]

I first met Carlos Fuentes in Paris, in the summer of 1969. This was also my first trip to Paris with Emir, getting to know the Paris where he had lived while directing *Mundo Nuevo*, the first Spanish language international literary magazine centered around Latin American culture. Emir had lived with his second wife Magdalena and their new child Alejandro on Boulevard Haussman near the pleasant Parc Monceau, a small and lovely park not far from where Proust once resided. Across the wide boulevard we went to a local café, where Emir insisted we have madeleines with linden tea, in honor of the great French writer. Even more than Barcelona, Paris was the capital of Latin American exile.

The Latin Americans with whom Emir and I converged in Paris were more Parisian than the Parisians. An outstanding figure among them was Edgardo Cozarinsky, the Argentine writer and film-maker and a true master of the art of conversation. Paris was also the home, as mentioned earlier, of the neo-baroque Cuban poet and writer Severo Sarduy who was also an artist, and his venerable partner François Wahl, the publisher of Editions du Seuil. I had met them both in New York months earlier, and François's first response (to my youthfulness) in May 1969.

The first occasion with Emir and Carlos was lunch at a Chinese restaurant Carlos preferred, in the fashionable 7th arrondissement, facing the imposing Church of Saint-Sulpice. He was famous for his tongue-in-cheek quips and I remember him joking that, because of the altitude, only Mexicans and goats had hearts strong enough to copulate in Mexico City. Over lunch when we were having lychee, a common Chinese dessert, he compared its taste and texture to the female sex, or, as he said in the vernacular, "tiene gusto a coño," and bristled his mustache in celebration of his proclaimed prowess with the ladies.

The son of a diplomat, Carlos was at ease with his role as an intellectual celebrity. While he claimed that you can't live and write at the same time, he was always on the go with both activities. When he was a young playboy, he shocked his patrician family by marrying a glamorous older woman, the Mexican actress Rita Macedo who often appeared in Buñuel's films. Carlos struck me as a bon vivant, but according to his literary peer Guillermo Cabrera Infante, Carlos had confessed that writing was a laborious and often agonizing experience. Despite this, while giving lectures all over the world, he published, prolifically, over sixty novels and volumes of stories and essays.

Emir and Carlos were key figures, it is important to underline, in twentieth-century Latin American literature because they defined a vital dialogue, stressing a shared new literary language, between North and South America at a very difficult time during the Cold War. These two friends had worked shoulder to shoulder to promote new writers like García Márquez in the 1960s by featuring

Figure 9.1 Jill (back to camera), Carlos Fuentes, and Emir at the UN, New York City, Oct. 1973. (The photographer is unknown)

them in *Mundo Nuevo* which, for example, debuted *Cien años de soledad* in 1966.

Literature and politics were uneasy bedfellows in the North–South context, and though *Mundo Nuevo* provided a wide-reaching venue for dialogue, Carlos Fuentes "diplomatically" stepped away from the journal to maintain good relations with Cuba's cultural ministry while still remaining Emir's friend. Upon Emir's death in 1985, Carlos wrote respectfully and with affection, omitting any mention of discord, that the "late Uruguayan critic and biographer Emir Rodríguez Monegal" had introduced the concept that the new novelists had in common one "Babelic" language, ranging from pop culture to pre-Columbian hieroglyphs, and that they were following the great avant-garde poets such as Huidobro, Vallejo and Neruda, forging a newfound literary Latin America in the twentieth century.

After Paris, Emir and I next saw Carlos in February, 1970, in an apartment on Central Park West, where Carl Brandt threw a party in his honor. An important literary agent in New York at that time, the burly, dashing Carl counted among his guests Rip Torn and, highball in hand, Lillian Hellman, who was holding court with a loud slurring voice as I stepped inside after leaving my raccoon coat in the hands of Carl's attractive wife. As Emir steered me into the living room, Rip Torn approached to speak with us briefly, but I quickly realized he was orbiting the chic scene with a leer for the ladies including, for one second, me. Now in the center of the room we glimpsed Shirley MacLaine, seated on a sofa next to Carlos, on whose other side sat his latest flame, a glamorous young Mexican woman with green eyes named, I would learn, Carla Stellweg, who welcomed me with a smile. For years afterward, at Latin American events, Carla and I would greet each other with warm embraces as if we were bosom buddies.

Carlos greeted us both, rising to hug his Uruguayan friend Emir. Resplendent in a slinky top and silky party slacks I wore to cover the cast on my left leg—both fibula and tibia were broken in a skiing accident in Vermont a month earlier—and accessorized by a shiny black cane for which I received sympathetic glances. The waters were divided, a place was made for me on the nearest corner of the twin sofa, and I plopped down facing Carla, Carlos and Shirley.

Snuggly next to me sat a famous and very tall Danish couple, Eberhard and Phyllis Kronhausen, who had recently published a coffee table bestseller called *Erotic Fantasies*, amply illustrated with explicit photos on the risqué topic which I recall vaguely as "staying young by indulging in lots of sex."

Apropos of that book, it is possible that Carlos introduced me at the party as the Lolita of the Boom—a questionable accolade. Carlos continued to call me this on more than one occasion, in part celebrating my still relatively young age when I translated his novella as part of an outrageous trio of explicit homosexual works of fiction published under the unfortunate title of *Triple Cross*, but the main reason I suppose was Emir and myself in coupledom, with twenty-five years between us. Neither Emir, a Yale professor and distinguished literary critic with his Latin Svengali dark thick eyebrows, nor I took the matter too seriously, though, in hindsight, I see the negative side of how Carlos and others perceived us as a couple, particularly regarding the judgmental or at least prejudicial proclivities of academe then. In other ways, from what I gather, the censorious atmosphere is worse now.

Back to the sex-happy Danish couple: Wife and husband were lanky white-haired Scandinavians, deeply wrinkled no doubt from long vacations in the sun but brimming with youthful energy, their wrinkles and white hair contrasting radically with their vitality. Eberhard's name to my keen ear suggested Everhard, especially as he was hitting on me, despite my cane and cast, right under his wife's encouraging nose. I reacted by leaning away, perilously shifting to the sofa's edge, and no doubt grimacing or uttering some wisecrack. I say no doubt because at that moment Shirley eyed me mischievously, apparently disapproving of my ill humor or, shall we say, lack of *savoir faire*. A bit later when she and I stood, this time across from each other at a copious buffet table, we two girls exchanged complicit smiles. I knew all was well, then, and could feel a casual comradery vis-à-vis friendly but lecherous Eberhard.

Carlos was an irrepressible name-dropper (as if I weren't) like the time when Emir and I were in New York visiting Cabrera Infante at the loft apartment of his good friend Nestor Almendros, and a phone call from Carlos explained that he could not see Guillermo in New York because he was spending the weekend at the house of William (and Rose) Styron in Martha's Vineyard. Carlos sometimes went a little overboard, as when he dedicated one of his books to his "friend Shirley MacLaine on Sheridan Square, under an umbrella in the rain." He was perhaps his most important character, as when he published a so-called reportage in *The New York Times Magazine* about the May 1968 revolutionary demonstrations in Paris as if he had been a witness, in the thick of it along with Jean Genet. We soon learned that he had been safely at home in Mexico at the time, and when queried about this discrepancy he said, "Well, isn't all writing fiction?"

In 1971, Carl Brandt and an editor at Dutton asked me to translate Carlos's novella *Zona sagrada*, based on the relationship between Mexican actress Maria Felix and her gay son, given the fictional name "Mito" or Myth. When translating the torturous prose of the novella, I was able to feel the truth of what Cabrera Infante said about the author's struggle with writing—in its hallucinatory narrative and mythical allusions in which Mito is a modern-day avatar of Homer's Telemachus, it was a little overdone. Taking place in both Mexico City and on the Amalfi Coast, *Holy Place* came out in 1972 in the volume of three novellas with the aforementioned lame title.

In promoting this project, Carlos was not only seeking a venue for his offbeat story but supporting two other writers, lesser known, including the gay Cuban exile Severo Sarduy's novella *De donde son los cantantes* ("From Cuba with a Song") and *El lugar sin límites* ("Hell Has No Limits") by Carlos's boyhood friend, José Donoso. Nicknamed "Pepe," the charming Chilean was a keen wit, bitchy but also fragile health-wise. With "La Manuela," an effeminate gay cross-dresser as the principal character in a rural brothel, the novella *Hell Has No Limits* was a courageous work in Latin America in the mid-1960s.

As these were short works, Carlos had proposed the project to publish in one volume all three novellas. His initial purpose, again, was to feature his own neo-baroque *Zona sagrada* underlining the subversive eroticism of Mexican and mythological goddesses from the Greeks to the Aztecs. The mythic content framed the real and unhealthy relationship between Mexican diva Maria Felix and her gay son. Carlos had wanted to call the three-volume book "The Baudyville Trio," which is closer to the carnivalesque spirit of these novellas and certainly better than the misnomer *Triple Cross*. Chosen by our Dutton editor intending to allude to Catholicism as well as cross-dressers, the title sounded like a political thriller, and hence was misleading, sending the wrong signal to its potential audience which would consist of readers open to rare, gender-bending literary texts. Readers might have understood the Catholic association with "three in one" of "Triple" as well as the obvious "Cross" allusion. But the word "Cross" was farfetched in trying to stress a subversive juxtaposition of the sacred and the profane. *Zona sagrada* meant literally "sacred zone" but at the time, the more resonant *Holy Place* was an emphatic wink toward the sacrilegious effect sought by the author.

*

Not as opaque as the other two works, Pepe's novella was a dazzling and engaging portrayal of a grotesque yet tragic gay figure and the brutal circumstances of life in a rural brothel. It became a Mexican film, directed by Arturo Ripstein with a screenplay by Manuel Puig. Its title, *Hell Has No Limits* (*El lugar sin limites*, originally the phrase "Hell hath no limits") is borrowed from Christopher Marlowe's *Doctor Faustus*.

I spent over a year translating the three novellas. The most obscure of the unholy threesome was by Severo Sarduy, Cuban poet, painter and novelist, whose 1967 *De donde son los cantantes* (literally "where are the singers from") is an intricate and multilayered parody of Cuban history as represented by three cultures or ethnicities, originally from Spain, Africa and China, the latter mostly in one section of Havana, having immigrated to Cuba during the Boxer Rebellion. The Chinese chapter struck scholars as the most fanciful aspect of Sarduy's personal "anthropology" of Havana, but this witty (to those who got the jokes) and neo-baroque text brings together not only popular and high cultures but also East and West in the creation of Cuba's identity. *From Cuba with a Song*, a title arrived at after much rumination, alluded to a famous folksy Cuban song with Afro-Cuban elements. But Marxist Cuba is also parodied in Sarduy's pop portrait of Cuba, hence my choice of title intentionally recalls James Bond's *From Russia with Love*, made sense within this queer, "pop" and rococo representation of Cuban history.

Over several years I would translate four novels by Sarduy, one more impossible than the next. I think my favorite might be *Maitreya*, a ribald version of the metamorphoses of the boy who becomes the future Buddha, and, at the same time, a hallucinatory depiction of the Chinese invasion of Tibet. Decades after his death in 1993, Sarduy still has a small but impassioned following. Like his friend Manuel Puig but with a Caribbean flair, Severo, like the *rumbera* maid in *The Birdcage* was out to all his friends.[18]

Donoso, from a slightly older generation, was bisexual, perhaps leaning more to the gay side. With his first novel *Coronation* in 1962, awarded a Faulkner Foundation prize, Donoso became a leading novelist in Chile. For his superb stories and novels, he received Guggenheim fellowships and in 1990 was awarded the Chilean National Prize for Literature. About his ambitious novel *The Obscene Bird of Night*, which came out in 1973, Robert Coover wrote in the *New York Times*, "this is a dense and energetic book, full of terrible risk-taking ... that deserves its place among the major works of Asturias and Fuentes, Cortázar and Rulfo, Vargas Llosa and García Márquez."[19] John hailed another long novel (which I co-translated) *House in the Country*—a feverish allegory of Chile under Pinochet's dictatorship—as a postmodernist masterpiece.[20] Aside from fiction, Donoso wrote his own controversial "moveable feast" memoir, as mentioned earlier, *A Personal History of the Boom*. He was frequently in New York and taught creative writing at Princeton and at the Iowa Writers' Workshop in the mid-1960s before he moved to Spain. He would not return to Chile until the fall of Pinochet in 1983.

Pepe, as his friends called him, visited me in 1993 in Santa Barbara where we recorded an interview. Like Carlos, Pepe had been amazed that at a young age I had taken on the three decadent and difficult novellas. Pepe was a kind friend, supportive after Emir's death and on that visit, he wanted to hear about my life and to share confidences, and even, like Guillermo, to give me advice about the tribulations of love relationships.

*

Aside from Barcelona, Emir and I met with Pepe and his lively, deep-voiced spouse Maria Pilar in New York around the Christmas holidays in the early 1970s, a festive occasion at the apartment of his good friend Kurt Vonnegut in the West Village. Years later, when I was in Santiago, Chile in 1991, Pepe invited me to a family luncheon where, just like in the summer of 1973 when I attended a Parisian midday feast with Bioy, Silvina and family, I felt an outsider not only as a non-family guest but, in terms of class difference, by wealth. In both cases upper-class attitudes at the long table of family members were off-putting. In both situations, the younger relatives seemed oblivious to the achievements of the major writer or writers in their family.

Back to 1970, that summer, now that I was liberated from the cast on my leg, Emir and I rented a SEAT, a mini car similar to the Fiat, to take a trip around Spain. I was the driver as Emir, who presciently saw the automobile industry as America's downfall and was an urbanite 100 percent or *cien por cien*, never deigned to learn. From Madrid we set out for an exquisite hilltop castle inn or *parador* midway to Valencia by the sea. The next day we followed the coast up to Barcelona, where we visited the brothers Juan and Luis Goytisolo in their respective country estates, with their respective wives, in the region of Tarragona.

As Catalans, initially both Juan and Luis opposed Franco's Spain and traditional Castilla. Juan's novels were biting critiques of Franco, which is why he had left Spain to live in Paris, where he worked as the Spanish-language acquisition editor for Gallimard, and became close friends with fellow gay exile from Cuba, Severo Sarduy. In the early 1980s I translated excerpts from novels of both Luis and Juan for the *Triquarterly* magazine's special issue on Spanish writing from mid-to-late twentieth century. At Juan's house, where he and his French spouse Monique were spending the summer, we learned that the Goytisolo family wealth had come from turn-of-the-century Cuba, where their grandfather had owned sugar mills.

In our conversation during that visit, Juan recognized the irony of his capitalist background, considering his fervent support of the Cuban Revolution. It was a pleasant afternoon, having an aperitif on a rustic terrace and viewing the countryside, with Juan and the charming Monique Lange, who was also a fine novelist. I was intrigued because Juan was openly gay, and therefore this seemed to me a *mariage blanc*. Years later Manuel Puig spoke to me of another such arrangement involving his friend Paloma Picasso, daughter of the painter and Françoise Gilot, married to a gay Argentine designer who lived with his male lover, forming an amiable *ménage à trois*.

*

In Barcelona we stayed at a wonderful old art nouveau hotel, the Rotonda— which was converted into a hospice a few years later—where Pepe Donoso came to meet us. He invited us to lunch at his house in the hills overlooking Barcelona where we met his brilliant consort Maria Pilar and caught a glimpse of their only and adopted daughter whose nickname was Pilarcita, a little girl then, and Pepe's beloved pug, whom he called Peregrine Pickle. Like most pugs, this one notably snorted in fits and starts, a sound that punctuated the lively conversation which included Pepe's concerns about Peregrine Pickle's respiratory health. Many years later, their daughter, like her mother named Maria Pilar (to whom both Pepe and his wife seemed devoted) would publish in Spain the "true" story of her dysfunctional parents as she saw them, and shortly afterwards, tragically, committed suicide.

We saw Carlos later, during this trip, and this time Carlos had invited us to join him at lunch with the now world-famous Gabriel García Márquez, Gabo to his friends, at one of his favorite restaurants on the Ramblas. Living with wife and children in Barcelona, which by 1970 had become a safe port for exiled Latin American writers, Gabo was conveniently settled in the same town as his dynamo literary agent, Carmen Balcells. Gabo, who won the Nobel prize in 1984, acquired homes in Paris as well as Barcelona and of course in Colombia and Mexico.

Carmen was an ample, stout, bustling, tough-as-nails businesswoman with a great booming voice. She was very welcoming when I visited her offices decades later in 2002 while on a book tour, as the agency was involved with the Spanish publication of my biography of Manuel Puig. At that time, the agency was run entirely by a smart group of women and they also welcomed me with great warmth. It felt good to be in this brainy woman's world (despite the patriarchal Latin culture in the times of Franco) created by the charismatic and down-to-earth Carmen.

In our tiny SEAT 500 Emir and I picked up Carlos and Gabo awaiting us at an outdoor café; miraculously they were able to pile into the tight backseat. Carlos Fuentes's elegant appearance presented a sharp contrast with Gabo's. With his checkered shirt, dark curly hair and thick mustache, Gabo looked like a taxi driver, that is, a man of the people. At lunch on the lively Ramblas, I was struck by Carlos's generosity as a literary star himself who happily yielded center stage to Gabo, the new rising star as it were. With great panache, Gabo told jokes and anecdotes, and we three were his enraptured audience. To top off this splendid occasion, we all ordered Gabo's favorite dessert, *crèma Catalana*, a delicious crème brûlée Barcelona-style.

I had been following a path of study inspired by the first article of Emir's that I read a year earlier, an insightful analysis of "innovation and anachronisms" (1968) or "Novedad y anacronismo en *Cien años de soledad*."[21] Thanks to Emir's guidance, I wrote my M.A. thesis on this magnificent novel for Columbia University, and would soon publish it in Spanish; on the Ramblas that day was an occasion to seek wisdom, literally from the horse's mouth. I asked Gabo about the writers he had found most inspiring, recalling that he had spoken often of Virginia Woolf.

He told me his admiration for her magnificent *Mrs. Dalloway*, and "a particular scene, in which the main character is sitting inside a coach waving her white-gloved hand, and what struck me," he continued, "is that all you see is her gloved hand slowly waving." He then told us that this scene had made its way into his description of a dictator in the novel he was then writing, *Autumn of the Patriarch*, a difficult work to finish, under great pressure, in part because of the great success of *One Hundred Years of Solitude*.

I worked on Carlos's novella *Zona sagrada* the following summer, and we corresponded in the fall when I had finished a first draft. In one of his letters to me from Mexico City, written in November 1971, Carlos told me that I made him "read like Henry James." This felt like an exaggeration but I couldn't help feeling delighted by the compliment: James was a master of narrative technique, ambiguity and serpentine syntax. The collaboration with Carlos was very friendly, and our correspondence not only offers insights into his influences, but also reveals Carlos's firm command of English, as in this passage from a letter Carlos sent me, where he explains:

> I have only one basic desire: that the Claudia-Mito dialogs should be a lot harder, rougher, biting, more vulgar. As long as he narrates in the 1st person, the Jamesian tone with baroque overtones is just perfect. But when the mother and son engage in verbal battle, there should be (as in the Spanish original) a marked difference; Claudia, particularly, should be very bitchy and almost like a gangster in her speech, like something out of Raymond Chandler or Ross MacDonald.

This was excellent advice. Those sections were a take-off on the hardboiled American *roman noir*, not only Raymond Chandler but also the grittier Dashiell Hammett's *Red Harvest*, a model for Fuentes regarding style as well as its content of social and political corruption.

The dialogues of the gay protagonist's mother, Claudia, again were also based verbatim on the legendary Mexican actress Maria Felix. He would later write a play imagining a conversation between Maria and another Mexican diva, Dolores del Rio, who starred in a few American films. The son of a diplomat, Fuentes moved in elite cultural circles and had close connections, both professional and personal, with the Mexican film industry, which included his friendship with the legendary Luis Buñuel.

Our archived correspondence is filled with "enticing" tidbits as in this letter where Carlos takes into account the nuance that I was more acquainted with Argentine than with Mexican slang. His clarifications were crisp and witty, as in this answer to requests for a clarification: "Escuincle is the Mexican equivalent of the Río de la Plata's pibe or the Chilean cabro. From the Nahuatl excuintl, a very small hairless dog. 'Brat' will do." In response to another query, Fuentes writes: "Actually, Chole is a nickname for women called Soledad." He then adds, with trademark tongue-in-cheek: "Cien años de Chole."[22]

*

It wasn't until August 1973 that I met up with Carlos again, this time back in Paris. I was then back in graduate school, at NYU, and on this trip, as I mentioned earlier, I was on my own. Following Nietzsche's counsel to "embrace your affinities," I embraced romance with the infamous Bioy Casares. Encouraged by one of my professors, Antonio Regalado who had quoted Nietzsche to guide me (and to free me of the guilt I felt about my infidelities), I took the train south to Saint Jean de Luz in the beautiful Basque region between France and Spain to stay with Antonio and his family.

Back in Paris, I was to dine with Carlos and his new wife Silvia, with the caveat that Silvia was pregnant with their first child, and the baby was due any moment. The day of our appointment I called to confirm, and sure enough, Silvia was on her way to the hospital. I suggested we postpone, but, always the gentleman, Carlos insisted that I join him for a drink to celebrate while he awaited the exciting news. It is sad now to recall that the son born that night and their second child, a daughter, would both die young. They both grew up as privileged children, with perhaps too much freedom. In some ways, this dire denouement, which I learned about from Mexican and American friends who were very close to the Fuentes family, harkens back to Carlos Fuentes's view that living and writing are often at odds, or as he told Guillermo Cabrera Infante, he felt that he had to set aside living when he was trying to write. Maybe being a writer also meant that it was also very difficult to be present as a father.

10

In Key West with Reinaldo Arenas

Perhaps the most defiantly outspoken writer among my Latin American literary friends was Reinaldo Arenas. As a queer and as a subversive writer, Arenas had suffered persecution and two brutal years in prison until he finally managed to escape in the Mariel exodus in 1980. This was when Castro emptied Cuban prisons and sent all his "delinquents" to the United States.

Reinaldo Arenas was the last "Boom" (or "post-boom") writer I met before leaving my life in New York and Boston. As a junior professor I moved to where I could find the best academic job for me at the time, and so I headed west in the mid-1980s, first to Seattle and then California.

That Reinaldo got to be known to readers outside of Cuba, with the publication of his magnificent novel *El mundo alucinante* (literally "Amazing Crazy World") was miraculous, thanks to his friends in Paris, the Cuban painter Jorge Camacho and his wife, who managed to smuggle Reinaldo's manuscripts away from the oppressive Cuban regime that censored and, ultimately, would imprison Arenas, as the film *Before Night Falls* faithfully shows. Reinaldo's manuscripts had been systematically destroyed or confiscated in Cuba, and when an early novel was published in Uruguay, he couldn't even receive royalties as this capitalist practice was forbidden to Cuban citizens. In these extreme circumstances, Reinaldo Arenas was acclaimed in French before he was published in Spanish—except for the pirate edition in Uruguay. Defiantly he rewrote those manuscripts by memory, a herculean task, and those suppressed books began to reach readers, first in French, then in Spanish, English and other languages.

*

I was an assistant professor at Tufts University in the fall of 1977 at the same time I was already a known translator with several publications to my credit. During those first weeks of full-time teaching, I had hosted my first guest writer, Julio

Cortázar, at the height of his literary fame. Opposed in principle to speaking at American universities as a vocal left-wing writer, Julio graciously accepted my invitation at the same time he rejected the invitation of the more prestigious Harvard Spanish Department, on the grounds that he, a jazz aficionado, had come to the region mainly to hear Anthony Braxton perform at a Boston nightclub. Even though the talk at Tufts University was organized last-minute, Cortázar drew such a huge audience from all over the Boston area that there was standing room only. My new colleagues were impressed and, unfortunately, a few of them envious of my engagement with the Latin American scene.

By the mid-1960s several writers in Europe and the Americas who had originally and fervently supported the Revolution, were protesting Castro's severe Stalinist-style policies—censorship, widespread persecution of homosexuals and of poets and writers summarily branded as *gusanos*, or worms—curiously borrowing Hitler's demeaning label for Jews. Julio Cortázar however, loyal to radical left-wing politics, continued supporting Fidel Castro. Under the influence of his former lover, the Russian-born editor Ugne Karvelis who had taken over the position of foreign acquisitions at Gallimard, the idealistic Argentine writer refused to believe the news of the persecutions.

Rumor had it, tangentially, that by the early 1970s Cortázar had undergone hormonal treatment, grown a beard and joined the free-love sexual revolution. Exploring his newly-discovered sexuality to the hilt, he had left Aurora Bernardez—his first wife and soulmate of his youth. Their perhaps chaste relationship is reflected in his early story "House Taken Over." Two decades later, at the Getty here in California, I met Aurora, a warm and very intelligent woman who spoke the most beautiful Argentine Spanish. While Cortázar had a Canadian domestic partner when they both sadly died of an undisclosed disease in 1984, Aurora was the only one to whom he entrusted his literary estate, a wise decision.

About Karvelis who he had met at a publisher's dinner party in Paris, Bioy Casares remarked to me in 1975 that he had found her "heavy-handed." He described her as husky but was mainly disturbed by her aggressivity as a sinister bureaucrat, a Russian apparatchik. When I was with Bioy in Paris, we ran into Cortázar by chance on Rue des Saints-Pères, and Julio, as surprised as we were by this unexpected encounter, opened his arms, exclaiming "Che, Bioy!" and embraced his fellow Argentine in a ceremonious manner with the Argentine "Che." According to Bioy, this greeting was theatrical and not sincere, and Julio always made grand gestures in literary persona mode as if he were an ambassador.

Cortázar, on the other hand, commented (with a little envy I thought), when I first told him that I was translating him, that Bioy was frivolous, or as he put it *en anglais*, a "playboy." Both were born in 1914 (along with Octavio Paz and Nicanor Parra) and were considered disciples of Borges. Evidently there was no love lost between them.

When I invited Julio Cortázar to Tufts in autumn 1977, I tried to avoid the topic of Reinaldo Arenas but alas it came up, and I felt obliged to argue, in Reinaldo's defense, against the Cuban government's brutal persecutions. The brilliant Argentine, considered politically naïve by Emir and others, had swallowed whole the Cuban "official story" of trumped-up charges that Reinaldo had been arrested for seducing minors (a scene enacted in the film *Before Night Falls*) and in passing tried to hit on me, but I dodged his forward pass.

Cortázar did not budge on this fairy tale (literally), and it was obvious that we each, Julio and I, thought the other was brainwashed. As some of his provocatively ambiguous stories suggest (most famously "The Devil's Drivel" translated into the film *Blow-up* by Antonioni), I had a sense that he may have been uncomfortable with his own bisexuality despite his bohemian or revolutionary esprit—or perhaps homophobic as Latin American men typically were. In any case Reinaldo's real "crime" was that he was gay and also promiscuous—two conditions considered synonymous in the AIDS era—as narrated in his posthumous memoir.

Lydia and I met Reinaldo Arenas at a New Year's party in 1980 or 1981 in southwest Miami with salsa dancing and rum flowing, in a small apartment crammed with gay poets just arrived in the Mariel exodus. We were both struck by the humble quality of this man who was perhaps the most significant Cuban writer of his generation. He appeared to have the guileless simplicity of a campesino, albeit a well-read campesino. Reinaldo had been born into rural poverty in 1943 and would be dead before the age of fifty from AIDS in 1990 (after a friend helped him to commit suicide as he didn't want to die in a hospital). I had translated one of his stories, "With My Eyes Closed," a lyrical stream-of-consciousness monologue of a little boy, for the 1980 *Fiction* magazine issue of Cuban literature I had co-edited.

I never got a chance to translate more of his writing because he already had steadfast candidates, one of them Dolores Koch, a good friend of his who took over the task. And before the American publications of his work in English, he had been translated already by Gordon Brotherston in the UK, who had rendered *El mundo alucinante* and titled it *Hallucinations*. While this title was lexically close to the original, "mundo alucinante" really exclaims, in colloquial Cuban, "what a crazy world." The principal character was based on a real historical figure, a persecuted priest from Mexico, and thus the American translation which came out later was titled *The Ill-Fated Peregrinations of Fray Servando Teresa de Mier.*

Reinaldo was a curious combination of tough guy and effeminate. He spoke with a lisp, was a bit shy, and he struck me as a rough diamond, without the sophistication of fellow Cuban exiles Severo Sarduy and Cabrera Infante, both of whom had been living for years in Europe. A cultural gulf yawned between the likes of Sarduy and Arenas: Reinaldo was sixteen when the Revolution occurred and belonged to the first generation which had been educated almost entirely under Castro.

While in Miami, thanks to Lydia's aunt, I was able to meet and also to interview the legendary Lydia Cabrera, by then a frail elderly writer who had dedicated her whole life to studying and writing about the African culture in Cuba and Afro-Cuban syncretism. Ahead of her time, Lydia Cabrera, from a wealthy and privileged background in Cuba, had a same-sex partner for many years, quite outrageous in Cuba and Latin America in general, in those days.

I don't remember how Lydia, Reinaldo and I decided to go to Key West together, but, in that festive atmosphere of flowing rum, fast chatter and marvelous Cuban music, it didn't take much to convince the newcomer to join us. Reinaldo had heard of me and was delighted when he learned that Guillermo Cabrera Infante was a close friend and that we were devoted friends with Emir Rodríguez Monegal for whom Reinaldo was an important new voice in Latin American literature. With that astute literary nose of his, Emir had been among the first to publish a fascinating and informative essay about Arenas. *El mundo alucinante* still stands out as one of the best of the twenty volumes of fiction and poetry Reinaldo wrote before AIDS sent him to his death. Not only one of Latin America's most brilliant satirical novels, this work transcends the autobiographical to bring together censorship, repression and the history of political exile not only in Latin America but in Spain and European countries as well.

And so, the following day after the party, we were on our way in a rented convertible down the peninsula, crossing the bridges from Key Largo to Isla Morada and down to the tip: Key West. Lydia and I were staying in a very "in" gay hotel at that moment, "La Terraza de Martí," popularly called the "La Dee Da." The legendary Cuban poet and national hero José Martí had resided in that

Figure 10.1 Jill and Reinaldo Arenas on the beach in Key West, Florida, 1980–81. (Photo credit: Lydia Rubio.)

building, hence its name. From one of its balconies, he had given speeches to his fellow Cubans in exile at that time. As Reinaldo was on a stricter budget, he stayed, inversely, in a lesbian-run boarding house called "Carmen Miranda's Veranda." These playful names brought together Caribbean spice and Key West hedonism.

Our brief weekend of beach, seafood, refreshing beer, daiquiris and wanderings about that colorful funky town, included, of course, photos in front of the famous sign that read "90 miles to Cuba"—both a nostalgic and disquieting message for both Lydia and Reinaldo, their home country so close and yet so far. At night, after dinner, Reinaldo vanished into his own adventures, while Lydia and I went disco dancing in a bar that was opened to the warm night air; at one or two in the morning it was still so steamy that we leapt naked into the deserted hotel pool before retiring to our room.

During the day, at the beach, we read books and swam and frolicked in the warm sea; Reinaldo was in his element, lying in the sand just as Javier Bardem portrays him in the film based on Reinaldo's memoir (*Before Night Falls*), a devoted beachcomber. I remember that I was reading one of the Proust volumes, a little ambitious for lolling on the beach—and that Reinaldo, eager to perfect his English, was reading a new paperback edition acquired in a Miami bookstore, of Herbert Read's *English Prose Style*. We discussed some linguistic differences that were challenging to any translator between English and Spanish.

This weekend trip with Lydia and Reinaldo, especially the drive down with me perilously at the wheel, was a verbal feast of gossip and laughter, and the whole two days conversing intensely and enjoying our youthful bodies in the sensuality that one finds in the balmy air of the tropics. Ten years later Reinaldo, afflicted with AIDS, would be gone, a suicide he heralds in a final letter published in *Before Night Falls*: "Due to my delicate state of health and to the terrible depression that causes me not to be able to continue writing and struggling for the freedom of Cuba, I am ending my life … I want to encourage the Cuban people abroad as well as on the Island to continue fighting for freedom. … Cuba will be free. I already am."

*

Cuba is still not free, as Reinaldo had so hoped it would be. Freedom to be oneself, even in the so-called free world, is a challenge many of us wrestle with our whole lives. Despite my own wrestling, I like to think that I contributed to the lives of others. It is not hard to sympathize with Reinaldo's memorable words to me: "the only consolation is the sea." Of course, he had another consolation, shared by most of those who inhabit this book, the solace of writing, of making one's world, with all its kinks and quirks, known to others, and perhaps to future generations.

The End (but not quite)

Epilogue

At a Bus Stop on Sunset Boulevard

Before moving west where my academic career would flourish and, at the University of California in Santa Barbara, I would become a "distinguished professor" now safely retired, my closest non-virtual contact with Hollywood and the film world was my own sister. During the 1950s and early 1960s, my sister had been what they called a "day player," not on contract. In "The Case of the Vagabond Vixen" my blonde sister Carol Leigh, with her Lee Remick looks, played a guest role in this early episode of the *Perry Mason* series. *Perry Mason* was a TV institution for decades, the most popular TV lawyer drama series, a show that started in the mid-1950s and still airs over sixty years later. Carol is the first character who appears at the start of the episode, hitchhiking on Route 1 or what we call the PCH, short for Pacific Coast Highway, a road I have often driven since I moved to Santa Barbara to teach at the university in 1988. But in this early *Perry Mason* episode, the road looks rural, with barely any traffic. The first dialogue goes like this, after the driver, a distinguished-looking older man, stops for my sister who's waving him down:

The man:　"Hop in, doll."

My sister:　"Where you going?"

The man:　"Far, but not too far. How far are you going?"

My sister:　"Far enough." The man looks at her shapely knees. She pushes her skirt down and says: "But my mother said never take rides from strangers."

The dialogue belies the surface insouciance of the scene. She played a young girl named Veronica Vale (to alliterate alas with vixen) who was working with a blackmailer. While the word is never used in the show, the blackmailer was her pimp but in the 1950s they didn't say such things, too strong for mainstream television programs. Television was "cold" then, which means it was controlled by strict rules of propriety. So, we first see her getting into a car as a hitchhiker, the car driven by a gentleman who's a film producer and, we soon find out, she's an aspiring actress. So that's the role she plays as the blackmailer's moll, to get this film-maker into trouble with his wife; indeed, while my sister the "Vixen" is in his house, the producer is murdered.

In the dialogue her voice is clear, and she speaks almost as if she were British, or Grace Kelly, which reminded me of how, curiously, my mother used to sound quasi-British when she spoke on the phone. It was sort of like putting on one's Sunday best. Carol had to sound "refined"—without a trace of the native New York accent. So, my sister goes with the lecherous producer into the house, evidently prey to the old man's sexual aggression, but she seems impenetrable, as if feelings were irrelevant; after all she's a blackmailer playing a role.

In the climactic trial scene, she attempts, with pouting little girl facial expressions I had seen her make at home, to lie to Perry Mason, a young, stocky but sort of appealing Raymond Burr. Who thought of it then, but now one reads him clearly as gay: just look at those ties and his flirty chitchat with his tall manly partner in the law firm. My sister, demure, looking down, her face now sweet, almost adolescent, plays the girl she was inside, though she was twenty-five at the time.

Carol was fifteen when I was born, and she felt her place as the youngest girl child was usurped by me because, as a baby, I would take the attention she needed so greedily and desperately from my mother. Might a younger sister's craving for parental attention, and envy or admiration for her more mature sibling, my oldest sister Alice, as well as the complex intimacy of sisterhood, guide her toward the spotlight in a combative attachment to her sisters? Being the youngest girl was a lesser position to begin with, and now she, Carol, had lost even that with my arrival. But why am I, the baby then, so guilty about her to this day, when I was powerless? I loved, admired, feared, and at times hated her and, when I was finally mature enough, felt great pity and regret.

So, when burly Perry Mason corners her in the witness stand, she finally lashes out, justifying defiantly her blackmail activities: "they're all rich and have fancy cars, why not." And then she fires with anger, the same anger I felt and heard from her at home in those years, "Haven't you ever heard a hard luck story, Mister?" No longer addressing him politely as "Mr. Mason," she bravely shows her rebellious self, the real her, as real as it could get.

Sound of a gunshot—in the first scene again—then high heels clicking fast down a driveway. The pretty blonde is running, dressed in a tasteful white or beige dress—I'll never know the color because it's in glorious black and white. Carol Leigh, my sister, as Veronica Vale. At age three her blonde hair was cut off by her dark-haired older sister, Alice, who I loved the most because Alice was loving and caring, but here she is, Carol, twenty years later, starring in one of the first *Perry Mason* episodes, a girl who leaves New York in search of a career as an actress in Hollywood, only to become implicated in a crime, exposed by supersleuth Raymond Burr.

He was one of many men in power she encountered in her voyage from an obscure childhood to the sidewalk-tramping uphill life of starlet, who married the wrong man, a dancer whose career had peaked, like buying a stock at the wrong time, and one wrong step led to the next in her descent into illness, madness and death. Shirley Booth, with her trademark matronly look, a serious actress with her two feet on the ground, liked Carol and advised her not to marry the choreographer Ray Malone, a sexy Irish guy several years older, who danced with her in the Broadway musical *By the Beautiful Sea*—a minor show but a big deal to us—who was a dancer going to Hollywood, or nowhere. He died, an alcoholic, at age forty.

If only Carol had been an erotic militant like Colette, or like Manuel Puig, who revolted against normal standards for desire, and against sentimentality. But Carol wanted to succeed in the world of norms, and almost always fell in love with Mr. Wrong or with Mr. Right at the wrong time. She did not take care of her mind and her heart, and her body went to hell. If only she could have had Colette's esprit and say: "I'm devoted to that boy, with all my heart. But what is the heart? … It's more worthless than people think. It's quite accommodating. It accepts anything. You give it whatever you have, it's not very particular. But the body… Ha! That's something else, again."

Oh, to be hard-hearted like those French, like Garance in *Les Enfants du Paradis*— "c'est si simple, l'amour," love is so simple—simple for those who feel it's simple, but this sentence inverts the subject verb order which is already not simple when translated.

Over a decade ago, in Los Angeles, my cousin Barbara (frail of health alas, she died seven years ago) and I were in a corner café in the middle of hot, desolate Toluca Lake in what Angelenos call "the Valley" and Barbara remembered that Carol met Al Hopson, the man she would live with until the end, at a bus stop in west L.A. A nice man, a bit-part actor with a mustache, he played, to good effect, a poker-faced bartender at the Hyatt and is shot in a comedic scene in the film *High Anxiety* with Mel Brooks.

Al would care for Carol and was actually paid (we learned after her death) by Social Security to be her caretaker, until she died in the Cedars hospital where I last saw her. We hadn't set eyes on each other for eighteen years. When I saw, as I approached the room, a somewhat plump gray-haired middle-aged woman, I didn't recognize her until I saw her eyes. It was a shock. I left the hospital that day both relieved and broken-hearted. Even though, true to her wounded self, she asked too much of me on that visit, reproaching me and our sister and brother for not taking care of her as family should, the regret that I hadn't visited her once more to hold her mortal hand was unbearable. Her lupus had never been properly diagnosed, and several weeks after my one visit, she died of a heart attack in June 1991 at the age of sixty. People who are doing well in Hollywood don't meet at bus stops.

I can almost see my sister, born during the Great Depression in 1931 (she's listed in a public record which she, or perhaps an obscure agent, obviously "amended" as 1933) stepping off the plane in Los Angeles, arriving in her hat and autumnal coat in 1954 at the perky age of twenty-three, her mind filled with hopes and fears, in this city where you don't wear hats and coats like you do in New York. I see her several years later in black Capri tights, sunglasses and sunhat, waiting for a bus, reminded that she met her last man, as Barbara put it, the one who would stay with her until death, at a bus stop. Did you know that only 8 percent of the actors in Hollywood actually work? No, he wasn't handsome, he wasn't one of those pretty boys she liked but were not the marrying kind. She needed a human being, not a pretty boy pin-up, I thought in that conversation with Barbara, thinking that Barbara too would have had a better life with a human being instead of the brief marriage she had with one of those pretty boys.

Perry Mason grills Carol and the sweet innocent façade drops away as the enraged wounded tigress springs loose out of the cage: "Some people aren't born on easy street, Mr. Mason." The last you see of her she is still seated in the witness box, her head bowed, ashamed yet defiant.

Afterword

Young translators today—see recent features in the *New York Times*, *The Guardian*, and other major venues—are finally getting some of the attention we have always deserved, and they are repeating many of the insights I had over thirty years ago, except that now there is an audience that's willing to receive these ideas in fresh versions. Good for them. And good for the media for finally catching up.

We all are always translating, when you think of it, to understand—even in conversation when we are communicating in the supposedly same language. French was my first "foreign" language, but my curiosity turned to Spanish and the Spanish people, and I would have liked to have had the time to master other languages, like Portuguese and Italian, at the same level. With the ghosts of Yiddish past and other Eastern European languages left behind in time and space, the impulse to absorb or immerse myself in the Romance languages like Spanish, made sense somehow. The foreignness or alienating effect of language can turn words into joyous playthings, as it was with James Joyce and his Cuban reader, Guillermo Cabrera Infante. One could say that some translators bring to the surface how writers and translators are fellow subversives, fellow outcasts in their own language.

My "detour" among Latin American literati, seen from this overview, had followed not only a desire for knowledge but also an affinity with the foreign or unknown, and with those displaced, those who as citizens of big cities like Buenos Aires and Havana, and later, Paris, London, New York and Mexico City, evolved into cosmopolitan spirits. After getting to know Buenos Aires and Havana, I realized how much these cities, and their people, felt familiar, at times like "translations" of the New York I missed or loved.

Translation, like writing, is a solitary but not necessarily a lonely task; I have often felt the writer there with me, engaging me in a dialogue. My first book about translation, *The Subversive Scribe*, wanted to bring to light the joy of translation by recreating in close detail, often with humor or with mother-tongue-in-cheek, the process of translating literary works from Latin America and how what seems a departure from the text is really a way into the text.

Unfaithful seeks to bring to its reader's attention a deeply personal view of the translator with myself as protagonist, aware of performance (and the ghost of an actress) as key elements, as if the translator were a picaresque character whose creative adventure is an erotics of translation. The translator is a lover; translation requires an intimate closeness with the text and at times with the authors themselves, a scenario in which there is, inevitably, a degree of unfaithfulness and distance. We need to understand that what may appear as a form of betrayal allows for the translator's subjectivity and her own voice to emerge in close dialogue with the original. We need to understand that the idea of fidelity is utopic, and that no literary translation can ever be completely faithful in a literal sense.

The common sense of the common reader (if such still exists) probably still holds that a translation is by its very nature "unfaithful" to the original, coined by the misogynist French epithet "belles infidèles" or beautiful but unfaithful women—or beautifully written translations are inevitable betrayals. The original is lost, always, like a loved one who is no longer. This prejudice about translation righteously justifies why some translators don't want anything to do with the authors they translate. If the translator is potentially at fault, the "superior" author has the implicit right to meddle with the translator's interpretation, even if the original author does not have sufficient command of the other language. The good news is, ironically, that translators, unlike authors, are not expected to be perfect. They don't have to suffer the "anxiety" of influence, because they are not supposed to be original. Which is totally naïve, as a real translator is an artist.

At its best, a translation plays two roles: as a critical interpretation and as a work of art that reproduces the original in a new form. The traditional raison d'être or ethical responsibility of translation is to pass knowledge and wisdom down the generations, but translations are never the thing itself. When I first began to cultivate this creative practice as a "closelaboration," what stood out for me was that certain authors themselves were keen to show readers that "what gets lost" is merely the flip side of what gets gained.

One of the truisms about translation—and there are many—heard over the centuries is that it is a "labor of love." An echo of Shakespeare's comedy of errors *Love's Labours Lost*, but even more to the point may be in Henry James's comment about how translators are miserably paid, or the famous cliché "lost in translation." The most critical epithet is perhaps the Italian "traduttore traditore," accusing the translator of being a betrayer, this pun first applied (apparently) to the French translators of Dante, critical of translators as traitors who dared to make over such a genius as Dante in their own image.

*

This chronicle of these writers and myself as a girl or young woman who aspired to create her place in a cultural milieu that still belonged largely to men, brings to light one woman's view of the 1960s, considered an era of cultural and socio-sexual revolution in the Americas, Europe and on other continents, a time of liberation. And yet we girls and women had to make our way in a society that, apparently liberated by the so-called sexual revolution, was still male-dominant, definitively pre-#MeToo. My "closelaborations" with male writers follow, somewhat, a long-standing tradition of literary women bonded with "great men" in which for women such as H.D., Simone de Beauvoir and others, love and creativity are part and parcel of an ongoing battle of the sexes. Has the #MeToo generation eliminated this battle? Maybe in some ways it has.

What is certain is that without the likes of literary figures like Jorge Luis Borges, Gabriel García Márquez, Julio Cortázar, Guillermo Cabrera Infante and Manuel Puig, it would be hard to imagine not only Latino/a or new writers in Spanish today but also other current protagonists in world literature. Almost all the Latin American poets and novelists who lit up the world of letters in the second half of the twentieth century are no longer with us. Assembled under the rubric of the "Latin American Boom" (for lack of a better term) some of them remain incomparable, a last hurrah—a good reason for this curtain call to feel their presence once again. Bioy Casares once quoted to me a poem by Browning that mocked the public's reverence for famous poets, "Ah, did you once see Shelley plain!?" Maybe to "see Shelley plain" was a lesser foible than others.

Acknowledgments

Over the years I have had the kind encouragement of friends, colleagues, editors, family members, fellow writers and translators, and my agent Harold Schmidt. Please forgive me for trimming the long list but let me note Linsey Abrams, Marjorie Agosin, Karen Braziller, Leo Cabranes-Grant, Cooper SY, Jorge Luis Castillo, Jeanne Heuving, D.P. Snyder, Danubio Torres Fierro (deceased), Janet Walker, David Lustgarten, Lucia Re, Bill Straghan, Susan Dalsimer, Sara Bostock and Victoria Tillotson. My gratitude also to the heirs of Bioy Casares for permission to use images, and to Lydia Rubio and Nestor Almendros for their photographs. And a special thanks to editor Amy Martin for her dedication to making this a final manuscript.

Grateful acknowledgment goes to the following journals, where some of this material appeared in earlier versions: *Words Without Borders, Another Chicago Magazine, Catamaran, Enclave, Letras Libres, Review (Literature of the Arts and the Americas)*. Thanks as well to Alejandro Varderi for his generous translation of early versions of "Remembering Neruda" & "Sketches of Susan" into Spanish, respectively for *Enclave* and *Letras Libres*. All unattributed translations in these pages are mine.

Work on this book also has been supported by writer residencies such as the Whiteley Foundation in Friday Harbor, Washington State and Ledig International House in Ghent, NY. My appreciation extends to libraries such as the Lilly Library (at the University of Indiana, Bloomington), home to my literary correspondence and translation manuscripts.

Notes

1 More recently Nicole Kidman played a UN interpreter in a more politically-charged film.

2 "Novedad y anacronismo en *Cien años de soledad*" (1968) in Emir Rodríguez Monegal, *Obra Selecta*, ed. Lisa Block de Behar (Caracas: Biblioteca de Ayacucho, 2003), 660–87.

3 Herrero-Olaizola, Alejandro "The Censorship Files. Latin American Writers and Franco's Spain". SUNY Press (2007): see Dec. 29, 1966, p. 97.

4 "Exorcizing a Sty(le)," in *Review* (NY, 1974), 61–62.

5 See my biography *Manuel and the Spiderwoman* (FSG, 2000), pp. 200–201 for these hilarious comparisons.

6 See my discussion in *The Subversive Scribe: Translating Latin American Fiction* (Graywolf Press, 1991), p. 85.

7 Manuel Puig, *The Buenos Aires Affair,* tr. S.J. Levine (NY: E.P. Dutton, 1976), p. 100.

8 If he made such a statement nowadays, animal rights defenders might protest, so I hasten to add that sex, of course, should only be with any living being who consented and not a minor.

9 Some of the letters here are to be found in the "Suzanne Jill Levine archive" in the Lilly Library at the University of Indiana, Bloomington. I have tried to capture their tone in my translations. Bioy hand-wrote all personal letters.

10 Quotations from Bioy 's correspondence in Spanish & English (translated by SJL) in SJL's private archive.

11 Keene was a translator from the Japanese who was clearly a literary thinker as well. I cite in *The Subversive Scribe* his making the "remote intelligible" which is an efficient and positive definition of what translation theorists call "domestication," which basically means "reaching out" to the reader.

12 McCarthy, Tom (2008). In his review of Jean-Philippe Toussaint's *Camera* (Dalkey Archive Press) in the *New York Times Book Review* (December 21, 2008), McCarthy suggests similarities between Toussaint and Bioy.

13 Paz Garro, Helena. *Memorias* (Mexico, D.F.: Oceano, 2003).

14 This conversation is quoted in the above-cited memoir.

15 From notes I took when reading a recent translation of *À la Recherche du Temps Perdu.*

16 See Donoso's *A Personal History of the Spanish American Boom* (Columbia University Press, 1977).

17 From Maarten Van Delden's obituary of Carlos Fuentes (May 2012).

18 *La Cage aux Folles* (1978), on which *The Birdcage* (1996) is based, was co-written and directed by Edouard Molinaro, one of Manuel and Severo's gay Latin American chums in Paris.

19 See *New York Times Book Review*, June 17, 1973.

20 See Barth's review in *The Review of Contemporary Fiction*, Summer 1992, Vol. 12.2.

21 Reissued in Spanish in recent *Obra selecta* of Emir's works edited by Lisa Block de Behar.

22 As noted above, my correspondence is archived at the Lilly Library in Bloomington, Indiana.

Selected Translations by Suzanne Jill Levine

2007 *Beach Birds*, by Severo Sarduy (with Carol Maier; translators afterword). Los Angeles: Otis Books/Seismicity Editions.

1999 *The Non-Fictions of Jorge Luis Borges*. Viking Penguin (edited by E. Weinberger; collaboration with EW and E. Allen.)

1995 *Christ on the Rue Jacob*, by Severo Sarduy (with Carol Maier), San Francisco: Mercury House.

1994 *The Selected Stories of Adolfo Bioy Casares*. New Directions.

1992 *A Russian Doll and Other Stories*, by Adolfo Bioy Casares. New York: New Directions, Inc.

1991 *Unravelling Words & the Weaving of Water* (collaboration/Eliot Weinberger), by Cecilia Vicuña. St. Paul, MN: Graywolf Press.

1991 *Tropical Night Falling*, by Manuel Puig. New York: Simon & Schuster; London: Faber & Faber, Inc., 1992.

1990 *Larva* (collaboration/R. Francis), by Julián Ríos. Dalkey Archive Press (Illinois).

1989 *Adventures of a Photographer in* La Plata, by Adolfo Bioy Casares. New York: E. P. Dutton; 1991 Penguin USA; London: Bloomsbury.

1987 *Maitreya* by Severo Sarduy. New Hampshire: Ediciones del Norte.

1984 *Infante's Inferno*, by Guillermo Cabrera Infante. New York: Harper & Row; paperback, Avon Books, 1985; London: Faber & Faber, 1987.

1984 *A House in the Country*, by José Donoso, in New York: Alfred A. Knopf; paperback, Random House, 1985.

1978 *Asleep in the Sun*, by Adolfo Bioy Casares. New York: Persea Books; reprint: Dutton, 1989.

1978 *View of Dawn in the Tropics* by Guillermo Cabrera Infante. New York: Harper & Row; two paperback reprints.

1976 *The Buenos Aires Affair* by Manuel Puig. New York: E. P. Dutton, 1976; reprint: Random House, 1980; London: Faber & Faber 1989. New edition: Dalkey Archive Press, 2010.

1975 *Cobra* by Severo Sarduy. Foreword by SJL. New York: Dutton.

1975 *A Plan for Escape* by Adolfo Bioy Casares. New York: Dutton; reissued by Graywolf Press, 1988.

1973 *Heartbreak Tango* by Manuel Puig. New York: E. P. Dutton; three paperback reprints: Dutton; Random House; Dutton, 1988. Forthcoming edition: Dalkey Archive Press, 2009.

1973 *All Fires the Fire*, short stories by Julio Cortázar. New York: Pantheon; paperback, 1988.

1972 *Triple Cross*: a volume of three novellas: *Hell Has No Limits*, by José Donoso (reissued) Sun & Moon Press, 1996; *Holy Place*, by Carlos Fuentes (paperback reprint by FSG); *From Cuba with a Song* by Severo Sarduy. New York: E. P. Dutton; reissued, Sun & Moon Press, 1994.

1971 *Betrayed by Rita Hayworth*, by Manuel Puig. E. P. Dutton; three paperback reprints (Avon; Random House; Dutton, 1988). Forthcoming edition: Dalkey Archive Press, 2009.

1971 *Three Trapped Tigers* (collaboration) by Guillermo Cabrera Infante. New York: Harper & Row; paperbacks: Harper & Row; Avon Books, 1985, Faber & Faber, 1990.

About the Author

Distinguished Professor Emerita and Guggenheim Fellow, Suzanne Jill Levine's books include *The Subversive Scribe: Translating Latin American Fiction* (Graywolf, reissued by Dalkey Archive) and *Manuel Puig & the Spiderwoman: His Life and Fictions* (FSG, Faber & Faber, UWP, e-book). A noted translator, poet and scholar whose prolific literary and academic career began in the early 1970s, she is the 2024 winner of the PEN/Ralph Manheim Award for lifetime achievement in translation, and she has translated over forty volumes of Latin American fiction. Editor and co-translator of the five-volume paperback series of Jorge Luis Borges's poetry and non-fictions for Penguin classics, her recent translation of Guadalupe Nettel's *Bezoar and Other Unsettling Stories* was shortlisted for the 2021 Oxford-Weidenfeld Prize.

Index

The letter *f* after an entry indicates a page with a figure.